Home from Home

ISBN:978-1-7967-5631-9 (print)
ASIN: B07NNP2478 (e)

Cover photo by Susanne Bacon

Susanne Bacon

Home from Home

Essays

For Diane

Thank you so much for stopping by! Best wishes to you, dear friend,

Susanne Bacon

Also by Susanne Bacon:

Wycliff Novels
Delicate Dreams (2015)
Wordless Wishes (2016)
Telling Truths (2017)
Clean Cuts (2018)

Other:
Islands on Storm (2015)

To Donald,

the cause of it all

Content

Food

Odds and Ends

Preface

When you emigrate, you are getting confronted with questions from all sides – from people of your former home country about how you manage at your new one, and from people from your new home country about how it compares to your former one. The thought to write a column about this topic arose, therefore, quite early. It took seven years, though, until the first article made it into a local online bulletin, because some thoughts had to settle and be filled with further experience. It is mere coincidence, by the way, that this collection of essays has been published in 2019, the Year of German-American Friendship.

Perhaps I was predestined to count amongst the emigrants of my family. Even the US as a destination were nothing out of the ordinary. My great-aunt Marta Keller made this journey in the 1920s, became one of the nation's first commercial female pilots, and gained renown in medical history when she prepped Albert Einstein's brain for scientific purposes. A few decades later, my aunt Isa Babb also became a commercial pilot in the US. I never had the desire for such high-flying adventures; but I made the acquaintance of a US Air Force member and lost my heart to him. I was in my late 30s back then and had a career as the editor-in-chief of a German trade magazine under my belt. Also, I had published poems and short stories, and I had a finished German novel manuscript in a drawer. It was only natural to continue writing, even if doing so in a foreign language. After my arrival in the US, I started hatching the concept for a column called "Home from Home". In 2017, I switched my citizenship.

This book intends to be no more (and no less) than a personal view of two nations. Even if some of these thoughts and impressions are shared by other German-Americans, there is no claim to general validity. And I'd like to tell all of you who flirt with the idea of emigration that down-to-earth fact books and rational pondering of your very personal situation are a better adviser than a book that is not meant to be advisory in the first place.

The articles of this book have been published in "The Suburban Times" serving West Pierce County in Washington State, between the summer of 2017 and December 2018. Each and every Friday I answered questions I had been asked at one time or another. I have tried on purpose to avoid any political or controversial topics. I wanted to point out everyday life differences between here and overseas in an entertaining manner. In the end, it has become a love declaration to two nations that are, maybe, way more similar to each other than you would believe.

Fests and Holidays

Carnival

My mother country, Germany, boasts of five seasons. Yes, you are reading right. Spring, summer, fall, winter, and – Fasching (pronounce 'fuh-shing) or Carnival. This fifth season starts on November 11 at 11:11 a.m. and ends on Ash Wednesday. The season begins with parades in costume, stage shows, and parties, and it ends with the burning or drowning of a carnival mascot. Ah, Fasching – as kids we were looking as forward to it as our peers here would have to Halloween! Its peak this year is reached next Thursday with almost a full week of celebrations.

You have business partners in Germany's Rhineland? Don't even try to call them on the phone during these days. Most offices will be officially closed, as everybody will be celebrating in the streets, in ballrooms and banquet halls, at pubs, and in private homes. People will be wearing imaginative costumes, often enough home-made in tedious, insane hours of work, just to be seen for this one seasonal climax of partying. Though we never lived in the Rhineland, I remember that my mother put in hours of sewing the most beautiful costumes for my brother and me. And didn't we wear them with pride?!

Along with Fasching came Berliner (pronounce bear-'lee-nah, no plural), kind of a fist-sized doughnut hole thickly covered with sugar and filled with jam. My mother used to make them herself as so many other Germans, and the house was filled with the smell of hot fat for days. The radio played carnival hits from dusk till dawn. Television broadcasts from

Mannheim, Mainz, Cologne, and Duesseldorf brought giant parade floats and the glamorous dance of Funkenmariechen (pronounce 'foong-can-muh-reeh-hun), a baroque military-style variant of cheerleaders, into our living room. Comedians on stage took up topics of everyday life to ridicule them in every aspect. And the more political shows paid it back to politicians of all parties – and those often sat in the audience and clapped at their own dismounting.

There was no trick or treating involved in German carnival. And only the boldest, little gangs of usually at least three or four kids held long paper ribbons across the road to stop cars for a handful of pennies. If a driver complied, those kids would make sure that their paper ribbons ended up around the car antenna to decorate the vehicle. If not ... well, the next one might oblige.

Today, I wonder how much or little I was aware as a child of the background of Fasching, Fastnacht, or Carnival. Probably as much or as little as kids here are of that of Halloween. I'm sure that my mother explained to us kids the more sinister masks of our home region served the attempt to chase away winter. And why on Ash Wednesday catholic classmates were permitted to come to school an hour late – they had gone to church while we Protestants had been doing our part of penitence over math books. Their absence and then quiet slipping in, one by one, made the end of the fifth season somewhat mystical. I also knew that Ash Wednesday started off lent.

16

I probably learned only later that masks and costumes were originally meant to cover up debauchery of all kinds during these days, especially that of people who had a reputation to lose. I only recently learned that the French Revolution's call for "égalité, liberté, fraternité" creates an acronym for the German word "elf" or 11. And, of course, rich or poor, high or low would be equalized behind masks. More or less.

Obviously, many new layers have been added to the original medieval carnival in Germany. Just as Zombies are enhancing Halloween over here, the customs of washer women of the early 1800s, of puppet theaters, of Guggenmusik (pronounce 'goo-gen-moo-'zeek, i.e. elaborately costumed marching bands), and maybe right now something new I haven't yet heard of are keeping the lively, loud, and lighthearted festival on the move.

Looking at some pictures, I realize that my very first Fasching back in Germany and my very first Halloween over here had two things in common: I wore tall hats. And I still don't like deep-fried sweet yeast dough – call them Berliner or doughnuts.

Valentine's Day

The first time I became aware there was something like Valentine's Day was when I was six or seven and able to read. I remember entering a flower store decorated all over with red hearts, and I asked my mother what it was all about. She told me that it was a day to give flowers to your loved ones. And she made it clear, immediately, that she didn't want any for herself on such days because it was merely a business idea. "If you really love somebody, you don't need a special day to emphasize it. You show it to that person every day." I was impressed. And I became aware of more – that my father, indeed, remembered year after year the day that he first met her rather than to observe Valentine's Day.

Valentine's letters at school? Oh my, that would have been a no-go! Some of my little friends received folded squares of checkered paper during school lessons that had been sent along furtively from one end of the classroom to the other (and you better didn't get caught doing that). How we crowded around those girls at breaktime to read the usually awkwardly written note, "I love you. Do you love me too?" It made us others giggle and a bit jealous – but also glad that we didn't have anything like that to tell our parents. A Valentine's letter to anybody? What an embarrassing thought.

Of course, times changed, and later, in my twenties, I'd have loved to receive a Valentine at one time or another. I never did. But neither did any of my friends. It was just something you heard about vaguely. Or you read about it in novels or watched it in Hollywood movies. Or you saw men rush to the flower stores after work to buy some red roses for their wife. I distinctly remember one occasion when I ran into a colleague of mine who asked me to help him out with some Deutschmarks – flower prices had more than doubled from when the store had opened that morning to when the husbands arrived in the late afternoon. Call that romantic ...

At one time in my thirties, I had the privilege to travel to a trade fair in Birmingham, UK. It was over a Valentine's weekend. I was staying at a fancy hotel near the elaborately restored Canalside, and the entire city had done its best to decorate for that Saturday's Valentine's night. As I entered my room, I found a gift from the hotel management. A CD with lovely lounge music (which I have kept and still listen to), a rose-scented candle (which I lit, and the hotel alarm went off – turns out it was not my fault, but a kitchen fire somewhere downstairs), and a flask of massage oil. Now, don't get me wrong. I appreciated the CD very much, and I have always loved candles. But when you are a single, nothing – excuse my pun! – rubs in that sorely felt fact stronger than a bottle of massage oil. It made me wonder how anybody who took Valentine's Day more seriously than I would feel about not getting a Valentine's letter in class that day, not having enough money to buy a gift like flowers, a fancy dinner, or even an engagement ring, or about being on the non-receiving end of such gifts.

I live in a nation now that celebrates Valentine's Day, and the stores have been decorated towards that purpose ever since Christmas Day (Yes, indeed!). I think my husband and I did the shenanigans with balloons, flowers, and a restaurant dinner twice. Then, I'd had it. Because I love flowers, but I don't want them because it is done on a special day. I like going out – but I dislike feeling rushed, crowded in on, and seeing people standing in line, waiting. I do get my flowers. I do get taken out. I receive a thousand tokens, big and small, all year long that show I am meaningful to the man I call my husband. It can be as useful as repairing something for me, as prosaic as planting vegetables with me, or as romantic as retuning his guitar to play my favorite song. Vice versa, I also try to see to it that he is not just at the giving, but also at the receiving end. Valentine's Day, therefore, is just a beautifully decked table and a fun, extra-special home-cooked dinner for us.

As a child in Germany, I sometimes found my mother shortchanged herself when she didn't want flowers on Valentine's Day (or, as a matter of fact, on Mother's Day either). Today, I feel like her. And in the middle of all the bustle about February 14 I don't want flowers or extra gifts as a sign of love. Because I just know ...

Easter

Passover and Easter have always been a very special time in my family. Though we didn't go as far as keeping up lent, the week before Easter in my German childhood went without candy of any kind, and Good Friday and the Saturday after were meatless. Church-going – German Lutheran congregations – was at the center of activities. Oh, and we had a two-week-vacation from school always. We didn't mind the former "program", we loved the latter.

Maundy Thursday was usually the precursor, and in many German households still is, with a dish of spinach, eggs, and potatoes – don't ask me why. As a kid, I hated and loved it at the same time. It somehow "rang in" the two Passover days ahead. I still keep up the tradition, and my husband doesn't mind.

Karfreitag (pronounce car-'fry-tuhk, meaning Mourning Friday) and Easter are the biggest Christian holidays in Germany, though most would deem it to be Christmas. They are also bank holidays; churches used to be well visited those days during my childhood – not so much anymore. I looked up the meaning of "Good Friday", by the way, as the word "good" seems a strange choice for the story behind. Indeed, the "good" in the day means as much as "God". Well, it's not easy to find church services over here on that day.

The first Good Fridays back in our times in Steilacoom, I remember I once experienced a real church service, and later it was turned into an open meditational church. Not bad, but somehow a far cry from a sermon and singing all those ancient hymns. The difference strikes me most, as a native German, once I exit the building and dunk back into a full-throttled business day.

I have to admit that I still miss the quiet quality of Good Fridays in Germany. Even television programs back in the day were muted down to biblical movies, Bach oratorios, and serious documentations. Discos were closed for two days. And in many German households fish was on the main menu. My mother used to poach an entire cod and dish it up with boiled potatoes, a luscious sweet and sour mustard sauce, and a salad on the side. Sounds like a simple dish, but it took hours to prepare, and it became rarer and rarer, as later you simply couldn't find whole cod anymore. I wonder whether it's a matter of convenience purchases that changed things in the food market to all-filets or whether cod was simply not as widely available anymore.

After two days of quiet (Saturday after Good Friday is business as usual in Germany), Germans enjoy two more bank holidays – Easter Sunday and Easter Monday. Church was on my family's program on Easter Sunday morning. Not the service at dawn, but the later one. By that time, we children had already had our Easter egg hunt and were pretty stuffed with chocolate eggs, fondant chicken, and sugar eggs. As we didn't have any garden and churches didn't organize egg hunts for their congregations, our living room was the hunting ground. It sounds like limited space, but the variety of hiding places was more than entertaining. I remember one Easter egg hunt at my godfather's house when we searched in vain for one hardboiled egg. It turned up a couple of weeks later in a big floor vase. There were no big Easter gifts in those days, except maybe an engraved fountain pen for on-going second graders. Ah, happy memories!

These days, I see lots and lots of Easter candy in US stores, even German brands. I might or might not buy some – we are not such big candy eaters, and the older you get, the more you rue the extra pounds you have to work off again. I also see these large prepacked pastel-colored baskets with gifts and candy. I wonder – do people take them apart and hide their contents here as well? Or do they simply place the basket in front of the expectant child? Whichever way – egg-hiding Easter bunnies are a curiosity that both my new and my former home seem to have in common. Even though business now continues as usual during all the holidays.

May Day

If on April 30 you find any of your German co-workers or friends a little restless, it might be because it's that time of the year. In Germany, they are celebrating Walpurgisnacht (pronounce vul-'poor-geese-nuht) and May Day big time ... and here there is none of this. Unless you are living in an area where German traditions are highly upheld. My guess is – not so much in Western Washington.

Back in the day, in my last German place I lived at, I used to participate in raising the May pole next to our suburb's townhall. It was a long debranched fir or spruce trunk, decorated with all the trades' symbols on the top and a beribboned wreath finishing off the colorful display. The fire department brought the tree along. Each year it was a breathtaking spectacle to watch, because the angles between adjacent houses it had to conquer until it was locked into its slot in the cobble stones demanded more than a few taxiing skills of the engine driver. The audience usually helped by pulling the ropes until the tree was up and safe.

After that, a tiny fair was opened – stands with regional specialties and all kinds of beverages as well as a beer garden for everybody. No age limits. Children chewing down on fries and burgers next to adults eating their steaks and having a glass of wine or beer. Usually there was an oompah band or a DJ, and people were dancing in the street until late night.

May Day is a bank holiday in Germany, also called Labor Day. Unionists use it for their demonstrations. The rest of the German population celebrates what is felt as the real beginning of spring. With hiking tours, sitting outside in beer gardens, having a glass of May punch, an intriguing mixture of sweet woodruff and bubbly.

Only a minority sticks to the darker roots May Day is associated with. Walpurgisnacht is a night when allegedly the witches are riding to the Brocken (which is a real mountain in the Harz region). Indeed, some people celebrate at the Brocken itself. Others wreak mischief such as unhinging garden gates or moving your patio furniture to the weirdest locations. It's not about destroying or stealing, it's about playing a prank on somebody. Still, if you want to be unharmed the night of April 30, you better turn everything moveable inside.

There is another custom during that night – planting a tiny May tree or pole into your secret love's vicinity and thereby declaring that she is cherished. It ought to have happened to a school friend of mine once, and she found out only a day after May Day. Her audacious admirer had somehow climbed the second floor of an apartment house and planted a bedecked birch shrub onto the balcony he had entered. It happened that the balcony belonged to an elderly lady who was enchanted that somebody had actually paid her tribute in such a way.

Ah, Walpurgisnacht and May Day – I feel myself getting itchy to join one of those May pole raisings once more and mix with the crowds, to sit next to a total stranger, listening to dreadful oompah music just because it's the thing to do. To chew away on a Swabian flatbread and have a glass of regional

Trollinger wine. To dance to songs from the 80s once the stars are out.

I remember walking back home on such nights, elated and yet anticipating havoc. And waking the next morning to what felt to be real spring, finally, even if it was pouring or cold. Somehow, the old Germanic heathen spirit might still lurk in me, I guess … if only for this tiny wrinkle in time.

Fireworks

It's this time of year again – Independence Day firework sales are soon beginning everywhere. Wait, not everywhere – mostly just on native American reservations. And possession is restricted as well. I'm not entirely bewildered by the concept. In my German past, there were restrictions as well.

Fireworks in Germany are also associated with big events, of course. Like a town fest – or one dedicated to fireworks as the Lichterfest (pronounce: 'leeh-tuh-fest, meaning festival of lights) in my hometown. The biggest firework occasion nationwide in Germany that comes to mind is New Year's Eve, by the way. The sale of fireworks starts three business days before the turn of the year. That's it. As a retailer you have to inform a communal office, and you can only sell specifically certified fireworks. Even gas stations may sell some – it may seem strange, but they also sell lighters, after all. Supermarkets offer huge boxes of colorful rockets and ground fireworks. Kids under 18 are not supposed to buy any, but I'm not sure how strictly that is controlled. And you are only permitted to set it off on New Year's Eve and the day after. That's it. I guess all the restrictions are one of the reasons why German New Year's Eve fireworks are so intense and long. The last one I experienced in 2009 began around 10 pm, peaked at midnight with an hour of extreme display, and petered out at around 3 am. It was mind-blowing, and since then I have never seen the likes again.

Over here, firework sales open in the remote areas of reservations quite a while before the Fourth of July – so-called alleys that consist of booths, often including a few stalls with food and beverages. It's a colorful display of basically one item in countless variations. It's bewildering. And you have to figure whether you are even supposed to possess any fireworks before you purchase. In our former home, there were stiff penalties even for just storing fireworks. Now we are living in a more lenient area, but we realize why it's so important to have a hose in the immediate vicinity of one's firework event, too. A few years ago, in our neighborhood a dry lawn went up in flames, and it was just lucky that everybody was outside on that summer night. Because there was no hose nearby, and we had to build a bucket brigade. The then empty house on that property never was in real danger, but the lawn, blackened and extinct, spoke its own language for the rest of that summer.

My first Fourth of July fireworks were gorgeous, if they only lasted about 20 minutes. The organizers obviously had destined each and every rocket to be appreciated for itself – and you were able to see the last fading of one before the next one went up, coloring the waters of the Sound with spectacular reflections. I loved that it was paced so slowly. It was hugely enjoyable. But it was over way too soon, too.

Well, last year, we went off to the Pacific coast for New Year's Eve. We had packed a load of fireworks. And we set out to the beach an hour before midnight. It was really chilly, and there was some wind. The beach was nearly empty, except for some other people with the same idea. As we set off our little fireworks (and before you can ask – we always clean up afterwards!), we saw the colorful blinking of ships out at the horizon. It made me think about all those who had to work that night instead of celebrating with their families. Of all those who had to observe GPSs and radar screens and tend to business instead of enjoying fireworks and maybe a glass of champagne. And I wondered what they would see of our small, scattered fireworks on the beach at all. The year before last, by the way, we simply slept through New Year's Eve. There is so little New Year's firework to be worth watching here. Maybe it's because there are *two* public annual firework events, not just one single big one as in my mother country.

I love to watch fireworks, though I absolutely dislike their sound. There are silent fireworks available these days, and I hope they become more common sometime. I don't get it that some people just set off these extreme booming explosives. It makes me wonder about how it messes with all those who ever went to war. And I definitely feel for all the animals, domesticated and wild, who must be out of their minds during these nights.

Yes, I'm torn about fireworks, too. But in the end, you might find me tear up at an especially beautiful rocket that fills the sky with a blowball, streams down in lavalike cascades, and finishes off with a rain of glittering sparkles.

German October Fests

October and Fest make for a pretty cool union in everybody's mind, don't they? They go with German beer, bratwurst, pretzels, Dirndl, Lederhosen, and oom-pah music. You might think of the Munich Octoberfest. Import it to the Pacific Northwest, and you have it authentically right here. Only ... you wish, but you don't.

Even for many Germans, the Munich Octoberfest has become so cliché, they leave it to the tourists, the VIPs, and the would-be ones who want to make it into the yellow press. My hometown, Stuttgart, hosts a similar event starting at the end of September (with a hardly smaller twin version in spring) – but the charm it held in my childhood is long gone. These days it's all about the craziest rides and about dancing on benches and tables in the beer tents. I've been there, participated, and gladly retreated. October fests of that caliber are not my cup of tea.

But there are other October fests that are very much so. Germany is not all about beer fests in October. For one, my mother country – just like Washington State – is fairly big, if underestimated in high quality wineries. Vineyard regions like Baden, Wurttemberg, the Palatinate, Moselle, Rhine, Saar, Saale, Unstrut, or Franconia (and forgive me, if I forgot a region!) feature wonderful Weinfeste (pronounce: "vine-fass-tuh") in their romantic villages and small-towns. They are usually announced with banners across the main roads and pennants spanning roof-to-roof all through town. The market place, usually in town-center, with a church, town hall, and most often the local firehouse, will be turned into an accumulation of booths of different colors and decorations, a band stand, and hundreds of simple benches and tables.

No entrance fees, no off-side areas for those who want to drink alcoholic beverages. You may have to pay a fee for your glass – you may keep the glass if you like it; you can also hand it back and retrieve your money. You get your food, your drinks, you ask whether the seat you'd like is free, and plop down next to anybody. You are a stranger to this town? You will soon be involved in some friendly chat in a local dialect. You will stay way longer than you had originally intended. You will taste local food specialties fresh from the oven, BBQ, or steaming casseroles.

Age doesn't matter; law compels vendors only not to sell alcohol to minors. Kids may sit with you as you are enjoying your wine or beer, though. Hours last till midnight, inside barns or other buildings even longer. Depending on the region, you may see different costumes (if any). You might listen to accordion music (not everything October fest is oom-pah) or currently popular music. You may see some dancing, traditional and disco. Some October fests even have a tombola, a merry-go-round, bumper cars, and a shooting gallery. But mostly it's about being neighborly, while celebrating this year's harvest with food and drink. Each village makes for a different backdrop at every single October fest, be it dedicated to wine, beer, cabbage, potatoes, or other produce.

As a German, I prefer authentic Washingtonian fall fests in Washington State. Their ambience cannot be reproduced anywhere else either. I love my Apple Squeezes. I'd love October wine fests, too – thinking some neat Washingtonian dishes, served with a crisp Wenatchee Riesling or a mellow Columbia River Merlot. Unfortunately, I have never run into an October wine fest over here. If you know of one in Washington State, would you let me know, please? I'm sure I'd plop down right next to you if there were seating, too.

October 31

Next week Tuesday is a red calendar day for so many American children. They have probably been figuring for weeks already what costumes to wear. Some will go to parties. Some will walk from door to door the old-fashioned way. Some will go trunk-or-treating in the safe surroundings of a local church. The rest of the week will probably be taken up with bellyaches and fond memories of that one night of trick or treating. Ah, Halloween!

Most people enjoy this special day. Even when they are just the kind of grown-ups who are handing out Reese's, hoping that, this year, more kids will show up at their door than candy-craving mothers with clueless babies in their arms. That they have enough treats to go around. And that nobody will ring at their door when they are already in bed.

Back where I hail from, Halloween has no tradition whatsoever. It became a fad when it came up in the late 1990s, and a few kids actually went around tricking or treating. But mostly, it was another opportunity for young adults to party in shocking gear. More like the utmost of Hollywood horror movie parties. Germans have a vague idea that the event hails from some English-speaking country. Most wouldn't connect it with druids and the Celtic Samhain fest, and they would not be able to explain what a guttering candle inside a pumpkin would have to do with All Hallows' Eve. In some regions the fad has died down again, in others it still continues.

When I was a kid, October 31 had a totally different connotation and, as far as I remember, was even a bank holiday. This year [2017], it will be celebrated in an especially huge manner. 500 years ago, in the beautiful small-town of Wittenberg in Thuringia, a rebel against Catholic church practices such as the sale of indulgences nailed 95 theses to the door of the biggest church in town. Martin Luther, 34 years old at that time, caused a ground-breaking discussion about Christian faith and, with his criticism, opened the path for what would be called the Age of Enlightenment. Standing up for his believes, he was risking his life. What remained is Lutheran Protestantism and a number of other protestant churches. We went to church to commemorate this event every Reformation Day.

Today I think it was a clever move of the former monk to post his thoughts to a well-frequented church on the night before All Hallows', as every churchgoer in Wittenberg would surely take notice of his protest. I can only imagine what an earthquake went through the congregation who had come to have mass said for their deceased loved ones. Not everybody was able to read at that time. So, word must have been spreading slowly. What would usually have been a very quiet church service would have had people whisper and pass on the message. From there, it would have spread to the first printers – Lucas Cranach the older, who was one of them and is also known for painting Luther, was one of the best advertisers for the new stand-off against the church of Rome.

Today, Reformation Day is hardly celebrated anymore. With the exception of its 500th anniversary this year. The day after, All Hallows' is a church as well as a bank holiday in Germany. Catholic Families will flock to the cemeteries and light devotion candles on the graves of their loved ones. As you can see, it is a rather solemn occasion, whether you are Catholic or Protestant in Germany.

Living here in Western Washington now, of course, I will partake in Halloween. There will be a Pumpkin Walk at the Steilacoom Historical Museum which I will definitely visit that day. And my husband and I will peek through our windows, checking whether some trick-or-treaters will pass by our driveway so we can hand out candy to them. But in addition, the Lutheran Protestant in me will celebrate the religious rebellion that was kicked loose back in the day. Solemnly and very quietly.

Armistice Day

This Sunday, we commemorate the end of World War I, Armistice Day. "We" as in those who still remember people who lived through it. Because since then it has been overshadowed by so many wars that seem to have hit closer. And the generation born at the beginning of this century might not even be aware anymore what happened back then. What is a memorial day for the victims of war in Europe, both combatants and civilians, is "Veterans Day" in the US for those who are serving or have served in the military – which makes the distinction between the two a bit more bewildering.

To be honest, World War I always figured less big in our history lessons than World War II in anything that my German generation was confronted with. Simply for the good reason that Germany had played a horrific role in it. As to World War I – what most of us remember is probably that some Austrian crown prince was murdered on the Balkan and that for whatever reason that triggered pacts between different nations to spring into action, which ended in a tremendous slaughter. We know about the trigger. We have forgotten about what were the smoldering reasons that set it off. We know about the devastation in Flanders. We rarely know about the families left behind the frontlines. What the British called The Great War has no such name in Germany. Probably because it left us very little. Which became one of the reasons for Germany's eagerness to win another war. I should hope that politicians over there are wiser now. The last war Germany won was in 1871 –

the only lasting result was the unification of numerous German kingdoms into one German nation. And I don't see why they had to fight France in order to achieve this.

On November 11, 1918 at 11:00 a.m. armistice was declared in Compiegne, France. Nine million combatants had died, so had seven million civilians. All over Europe you will find memorials for the fallen. When I was a child, WW II (!) veterans used to sell poppies in my hometown – I had no clue what it was about. John McRae's poem about Flanders is not commonly known amongst Germans for the simple reason that it is written in a foreign language. I haven't run into any German poppy vendors after the late seventies anymore. And did I say that I wrote my Master's thesis about WW I novels hardly anybody has ever heard about outside their respective mother tongue – books by Faulkner, Remarque, Ford, and Barbusse?

I grew up with war stories from WW II mostly. That is – those that were relatable. And, of course, we read, watched, and listened to facts, biographies, and memoirs galore. I was used to seeing veterans with empty-sleeved shirts and amputated legs. It only struck me in the late 90s that most of them were suddenly gone. The war veteran generation was simply passing away. Germany looked wholesome again. We shrunk from anything military. We turned obligatory military service for young men into something that was voluntary. Germany seemed to have learned its lesson after two global wars.

It is strange what impact these two gigantic wars still have on us today. I mean on a really personal level. Think where you would be now if World War I hadn't happened – and accordingly not World War II either. I'd probably be living in a Silesian small-town (because I love small-towns), if I had been born at all. If there was no American presence in Europe as a consequence of WW II, I'd never have met my husband and ended up here in Western Washington, changing even my citizenship.

Armistice … the cease of using weapons against one another. If anything in the Great War was great, I'd say it was these moments of agreement. Not just the bitter finale with such sacrifice on every side. I love to think of those moments when there was no shooting because the wounded were retrieved. And most memorably that unofficial armistice when Christmas united combatants across the trenches.

Armistice. Maybe in our everyday little battles we should simply cherish the fact that every person can create their own little armistices. And what if we even don't raise our arms against anybody in the first place except when we intend to embrace them? Maybe, that is what I take away for myself from what happened a hundred years ago.

A Pilgrim Fest

Thanksgiving is one of those wonderful fests that are celebrating a harvest successfully finished. The ancient Greeks had their festivals as well as the Romans, and I'm pretty sure that any culture with agriculture and livestock breeding celebrates another year of successful farming as the cycle is fulfilled once more.

In Germany, Erntedank (pronounce air-n-tah-'dunk, meaning "harvest thanks") is celebrated in early fall, the Sunday after Michaelmas. Church choirs and altars are decked with fruit and vegetables, and all the kindergartens belonging to each respective church show up. It's a family service centering on the children's performance, these days. Which also means that, due to lack of discipline, you often witness quite some screaming and running around. Most often, therefore, I rather took a long walk on German Erntedank Sundays, looking across the harvested fields around our suburbs. There usually were still some fields full of cabbage, pumpkins, or late garden flowers. I gave my private little thanks in silence there and then.

In comparison, my very first American Thanksgiving will probably always stand out as my most memorable one. It didn't take place at any family home. And it didn't take place in the United States at all, but in England, where my husband-to-be was stationed at that time. He had chosen a tiny Baptist church in the East Anglian town of Brandon to be his spiritual home, and he asked me to come along and meet his congregation on that very special day in that November ten years ago.

I remember it was an icy-cold night, and the room in the back of the inconspicuous little church was warm and humming with people. There were a whole lot of kids all ages, all well-behaved, playing with each other or sticking with their parents. The pastor and his wife had taken charge of laying tables and coordinating the buffet. Everybody found themselves some task to help with the dinner we would share. I was proud to contribute the brownies we had made at home the same morning.

Not knowing anybody was not a problem at all. Pretty soon I was in the middle of the happiest of conversations with people young and old. I wondered that there were whole families of three generations preferring to celebrate here at the mission church instead of their homes. That's when it struck me that the real Christian Pilgrim spirit is still very much alive in Americans.

We sat down at the long tables with people we might not really know. But it felt like we were united by our faith. The cold outside and the warmth inside gave us the sense of being a herd sheltered in security. And sharing the dinner made it very much like one of those biblical meals where plenty is left over, because everybody takes care to leave something for their brothers and sisters.

The buffet made it very obvious how wonderfully fed we are, and what a variety of dishes you can create from the same basic ingredients. Prayer and historical remembrance rounded out that deeply serious, yet also very serene occasion. We certainly knew that night what we were celebrating.

I have to admit that I came to love the American version of Thanksgiving instantly so much more than the German one. Maybe the history behind it gives it so much more specific meaning. The dire need in the Pilgrims' story makes it so much more palpable what it means to survive through Nature's edible treasures. I know that for a lot of people Thanksgiving is mainly a family fest with heaps of food. Yet, I appreciate even more the serious, yet serenely pensive variant of an American Thanksgiving. Such as that one on an icy-cold night in a tiny mission church far from home.

Advent

I guess it is pretty much the same for Germans and Americans – most of us love the Christmas pre-season that is called advent. Though most of us also don't want it around in the stores when it's still summer. Advent and Christmas carols have their season, and this year, when Thanksgiving is almost two entire weeks before First Advent, I certainly haven't put up any advent ornaments yet.

I grew up in a family that took advent pretty seriously, and I still remember these weeks before Christmas with warmth. My mother used to make her own advent wreath from fir, decorated it with red candles and ribbons, and stuck some tiny pine cones on for decoration. It looked the same year after year, and it was put onto the table only after Eternity Sunday. I have kept up the tradition of a home-made candle arrangement, but I have to admit that craft stores are a pretty awesome source for none-wilting, real-looking evergreens, and that my decorations and color schemes are changing every year. Putting up our Christmas tree before an advent arrangement has never been an option.

Of course, like every other German child, I received my advent calendar punctually every November 30. That was the day I was permitted to open the first of its 24 doors. Always one day ahead of the actual date, there would be no chocolate in it left on Christmas Eve … which made the distribution of the gifts even more exciting. As a grown-up, I preferred the Victorian kind of paper calendars that were and are still made in a suburb of my hometown. I like those best that integrate the motive behind the door seamlessly into the main picture. I had no expectation to find any of the like over here in the States. But I discovered a great variety of filled German-made calendars in diverse stores around the South Sound, and the Steilacoom Historical Museum's Christmas store even has a selection of those beautiful paper calendars. It seems that this German tradition has made it over here after all.

Come to think of it, a lot of Germans started to create their own advent calendars from various materials and in quite some quaint styles during the 1980s. Only the other day a friend of mine presented hers on Facebook, a row of 24 paper bags lovingly decorated with all kinds of natural materials, sprayed subtly with gold and other metallic lacquers and stuffed with little surprises. And I once helped fill and knot 24 parcels onto a clothes line that was to be hung into a friend's home. It's a fun tradition that heightens anticipation in people of all ages.

In many German families, advent is never (only) a church occasion. They gather around their wreath or arrangement on the four Sunday afternoons, having special cookies and other typical seasonal treats. Stories are read, music is played. Our family also always sat down and sang carols and hymns accompanied by my father's guitar playing. As on Sundays most Germans don't work, advent Sundays have an additional tinge of festiveness. Here, everyday life continues with its boisterousness, noise, work shifts for many – the

Christmas decorations inside and outside the houses cannot deceive about advent not being such a "biggie".

There is another German tradition that is upheld by many who have kids over here: Nikolaustag (pronounce: Nee-koh-louce-tuhk, meaning: St. Claus' Day). That is the only time Santa comes to German kids. On Christmas it is – a Lutheran tradition that made it nationwide over there – the Christ child who delivers the gifts. Santa stuffs children's boots that stand by the front door with goodies the night before his name day, which is December 6. These days, gifts have probably become bigger and more. Back in my childhood, it was just candy and dried fruit, and maybe a home-made sweet yeast bread in the shape of a man symbolizing Santa. My mother always made a braided woman with a skirt for me.

I am happy to say that American and German traditions perfectly intermingle in my tiny family's advent tide over here. My husband watches Charlie Brown movies with me – and they have become very dear to me. We deck the Christmas tree way in advance of Christmas, though we lay our gifts underneath only a couple of days or so before. I have to admit that I have never given my husband a Nikolaus gift. And I will have to hurry if I want to get him a calendar this year – they might be sold out by now. We do our rides around the neighborhood every once in a while, to see who has decorated their homes. And last year, my husband built a giant candy cane from plywood that he illuminated with Christmas lights. In Germany, I never had decorations outside the front door, except a door wreath. These days it's rather something on the front steps.

Ah, advent! We bustle like crazy to make everything as perfect as possible. There are social dinners over social dinners, Christmas tree lighting events, caroling festivities, Christmas movies, Christmas music, Christmas cards. It is noisy. It is joyful. It is stressful.

But my most cherished advent moments are still these Sunday mornings when we are sitting at the breakfast table and my husband asks: "Don't we have to light another candle?" And then, while I flick the lighter and the wick bursts into flame, we stare into the warm color and muse in quiet. How, as the year outside keeps getting darker, advent makes sure that the light inside grows.

Christmas

"Marley … was dead – to begin with." This line from Charles Dickens' novella "A Christmas Carol" used to kick off Christmas for me for many teenage and early tween years. I had wrought a tradition of my own to go to a theater in downtown Stuttgart, Germany, to listen to British actor Brian D. Barnes reenact the glorious tale of an avaricious recluse who gets converted to the real Christmas spirit. Every once in a while, my brother and a friend of mine tagged along to these unique, unforgettable productions.

By that time, Christmas to me wasn't really about receiving gifts anymore. Ever since I had discovered it was my parents who did the (probably carefully budgeted) Christmas shopping for us, I also realized that most of my wishes – except books and music – were flashes in the pan and basically a waste. Christmas had become something way more spiritual to me.

Of course, I don't deny that our family traditions of wreath-making and advent calendars were quite hands-on and less spiritual – but they added so much to the Christmas ambience in my little world. Or that of Christmas baking. And it seemed like my mother was cranking out endless streams of Christstollen, coconut macaroons, tube cookies, cut-out cookies, nut crescents, and whatnot. Our home took up the fragrance of cinnamon and vanilla, a sweet cookie smell that mixed pleasantly with the harsher notes of pine twigs in a vase in the living room. Advent Sundays were celebrated with a church service in the morning and caroling in the afternoon. Our family, always very close-knit, became even more of a microcosm during Advent.

Christmas time in German cities or towns is also unthinkable without Christmas markets and Christmas decoration. In my childhood, only few cities spent money on light chain decorations for their downtown pedestrian zones. Many were still filling in bomb holes from WW II or replacing temporary shacks from the 50s. The best decorations were always in the windows of toy stores, candy stores, and cafés, as well as department store windows. The latter displayed whole stories or scenes from fairy tales all along their fronts. When I left Germany in 2010, it had almost become something of a competition between cities about who had the most glamorous Christmas decoration, the biggest Christmas market with the most creative stands, or who could showcase the best choir, nativity exhibition, or extra-feature. My hometown Stuttgart's Christmas market has grown to triple its size ever since I was a child. It has even an ice rink on its central square, the Schlossplatz. The World Christmas Circus shows up on a fairground every year with "the best of". There are fancy exhibits inside the Old Castle, whereas in the castle's inner court choirs from all over the world vie for attention. Apart from that, each and every suburb has its own little Christmas market. Stuttgart's neighboring cities Ludwigsburg and Esslingen lure with baroque ambience, respectively a medieval fair as an add-on.

Christmas Eve, *the* main part of Christmas in Germany, always used to be a very quiet celebration for our family. Everything was scheduled, down to listening to specific radio shows in the morning that we gathered around for in the kitchen where my mother was cooking from scratch a lunch of the most delicious chicken soup and rice I will ever remember. After a nap in the afternoon, we almost always walked to church (over a mile each way) in a neogothic building with balconies and a huge organ. Our eyes would search the crowd for people we knew – and there *were* crowds back then. Extra-chairs had to be carried in, and people huddled real closely together in order to make room for more church-goers, some of them still left standing. No better tear-jerker than the ending of a Protestant Christmas service when the lights went down, the Christmas tree the only source of light, and the entire congregation singing by heart "O du fröhliche" (pronounce: oh doo 'fruh-lihe, i.e. O Sanctissima), accompanied by the fortissimo of the organ. After church everybody gathered around town hall to listen to and sing along with the local brass band playing hymns. Walking home through the cold dark made the simple dinner of weisswurst, mashers, and sauerkraut a festive warmer-upper. Then – finally – we ended up singing underneath the lit Christmas tree – a real one with real candles always.

Living in the United States now, my Christmases have changed, of course. My husband and I are mixing family traditions. Now *I* am the one baking cookies, and *I* provide the advent decoration. The Christmas tree goes up way before Christmas, unlike I've been used to from my former life, where it was decorated behind closed doors on December 23 to be revealed only late on Christmas Eve. We do rides around the neighborhood to look for the most beautiful Christmas lights – and it's quite interesting how close stylish and gaudy can border on each other. We participate in Christmassy activities as they come – Christmas at the Orr Home in Steilacoom and caroling at its Wagon Shop, plum pudding parades at annual dinners, Christmas stores, and bazaars. We attend church service on Christmas Eve. We enjoy a German dinner on Christmas Eve and an American Christmas dinner on Christmas Day before we exchange our three gifts each.

I would have to lie if I said I didn't miss German Christmases with its Christmas markets, church bells, hymns, and organ music. But my husband and I do combine the best parts of our memories and traditions, and we enjoy what we gain from the part that's novel to each of us. Quietly and in blissful harmony. So, as Tiny Tim observed: "God bless us. Everyone!" Merry Christmas!

Endings and Beginnings

Does this ever happen to you? You are watching a wonderful romance on TV, and when the protagonist couple gets engaged or married and "The end" pops up on the screen, you want to call out, "No way!" Because, actually, this is not an ending. It is a beginning, and the beginning of something much more meaningful, complex, and complicated than any courtship episode could be. But it's easier to just think, "Okay, so Darcy got his Elizabeth, and I don't want to think about the troubles he'll be running into with his terrible mother-in-law or whether he will ever be pushing a pram." Admittedly, an engagement or marriage is also what a lot of novels finish with.

On a more geographical note, confusion about beginnings and endings can happen, too. When I was living in Europe, the US West coast kind of marked the end of my western world – a logical thought, as in our atlases Asia is always depicted east of Europe. Now that I'm living at the west coast, when I'm standing at Cape Flattery, the most Northwestern point in the US (except Alaska), looking past Tatoosh Island, I am aware that though this seems to be the end of the world, across the water, way more west, lies … Asia. And I chuckle at my conception of former times.

Going for a hike here in Western Washington sometimes has me at the same point, wondering about endings and beginnings. When my husband and I drive towards the Carbon River entrance of the Mt. Rainier National Park, the tiny mining town of Wilkeson is the last fortress of civilization that you pass. Except for the ranger station further down the road and, of course, the loop to the town of Carbonado. Beyond Wilkeson, there is a wilderness of endless forests, waterfalls, rivers, lakes, steep mountains, and glaciers. When we return, again, Wilkeson is the first sign of civilization that greets us. So, depending on which way we are going, the beginning of civilization is also its ending, and vice versa.

When I got up in the morning of December 13, 2017, I left home as a German citizen. At about 2 pm that day, I pledged allegiance to the US in the USCIS auditorium in Tukwila. When I returned home, I returned as an American citizen. Though there was an ending in my life that day, it was a beginning at the same time. And it didn't interrupt my existence, for sure.

Pondering the concept of beginnings and endings, I start thinking that it is something that makes larger structures more conceivable for the human mind to have it marked by beginnings and/or endings. It's like cutting a roast into little bits instead of trying to stuff the entire piece into your mouth and chew it down. It's an auxiliary measure to grasp something more universal, whatever it is we deal with.

So, when we celebrate New Year's this up-coming Sunday – I wonder what we really celebrate. In Germany, we have gorgeous fireworks, started off by the midnight chiming of church bells all over the nation. It's goose-bumpingly awesome. And if you listen to or sing along with the traditional New Year's hymn "Now let's thank all our God", you have another tear-jerker that marks a very special ending … or beginning? Now guess, what German-Americans miss over here on the night of December 31 …

I remember when the year 2000 rolled in, and some people were arguing whether it was really marking the beginning of a new millennium. Or whether we should rather postpone our celebrations until the year 2001. And I sometimes wonder whether the entire count is right anyhow, for who can say that our Lord was really born in the year Zero?! Or was it 1?

Is it important whether we celebrate the successful ending of a year? Or that it's finally over and it didn't kill us? Or whether we greet the beginning of a New Year? Maybe a bit fearfully? Or awed? Because it is filled with another load of blank calendar pages that count down the weeks and months, and we have no clue what they will hold for us until they lie behind us.

Whichever you celebrate (and whether you celebrate or not), December 31 marks another round of endings and beginnings. I'd like to thank all of you who have been reading my little Friday column for the past months and for giving me feedback so kindly. I hope you stay with my ramblings about being "Home from Home" in 2018 also. This being said – I hope 2018 begins on a better note than 2017 is ending on for all of us. And if 2017 has been a good year for you already… all the better for you! Happy New Year!

Nature

Where There Is Smoke ...

Last week has left quite an impression of hazy skies, surreal sun-downs, orange-gray landscapes, burning eyes, breathing difficulties, and scratchy throats with many of us. Smoke was blown into Western Washington from wildfires in British Columbia, and I would rather not imagine what it must have been like there. Meanwhile, we have had our own wildfires at Chuckanut Mountain and around Darrington; they may have added but little to the extreme concentration of smoke. And as everything is parched due to lack of rain for the past 50 plus days, there have been burn bans imposed and lifted and probably, while you are reading this, re-imposed.

For a native German, this Pacific Northwest scenario is pretty awing. We hear of wildfires in Southern Europe on a regular basis. But we hardly ever experience them in Germany. As a matter of fact, the only one I remember was the burning of the Luneburg Heath, south of Hamburg, in 1975. It destroyed almost 31 square miles of forests, moors, and heath. For comparison: Germany's size is approximately 138,000 square miles.

My family had been vacationing in the Luneburg Heath that summer, and I remember my mother saying that if anybody dropped just as much as one burning match, the parched landscape would go up in flames like tinder. Well, a couple of weeks after we had returned home from quite a few hikes through sunburnt heath, withered moors, and austere, dusty villages, the Heath *was* burning. Arson, accidents, and incidents created a catastrophe that made the news nationwide. The fire lasted for ten days and killed seven people. I cannot remember anything similar in Germany ever since. And we certainly didn't smell any of the smoke some 270 miles further down south.

Meanwhile, over here and by last weekend, there have been burnt over 1,470 square miles in around 140 wildfires in southern British Columbia – almost 50 times the area of what burnt in Germany back in 1975. Somehow it makes me stop wondering that we saw smoke.

Only years later, I learnt that much of the extent of the Luneburg Heath wildfire was due to prior storm damages that hadn't been cleared and that made access to the seats of fire extremely difficult and dangerous. Added to this was a predominance of pine trees. I imagine this to be only two of the reasons why wildfires over here spread so incredibly fast and furiously.

If you ever had the chance to walk through a German forest and a Pacific Northwest one, the difference will strike you immediately. The rainforests here are dense, often inaccessible, without roads or paths, and of dramatic geography. They are enormous in size, and they are full of thick underbrush. German forests are nowhere as huge. In my small, but densely settled mother country, they are accessible through and through. Basically, they are seen to tree by tree. Sick or dead trees are hewn and removed; new, healthy ones are planted in their stead. Forest workers tend to storm damages quickly. It is doable pretty much anywhere in Germany. Our landscapes are comparatively tame.

When I smell wood smoke in Germany, somebody is most likely starting a very rustic barbeque. When I smell wood smoke here in Western Washington, it might be the same. Or somebody is heating a home or burning yard waste. Or something has gone badly wrong. As in a wildfire. Either way – smoke means fire. But the causes and sizes differ.

Total Solar Eclipse

The event was going to be mind-blowing. I was completely prepared for it weeks ahead. And then the day was there. I clocked out of the office, went outside, and watched it, totally stunned. It was incredible and unforgettable. Well, in a way, it isn't a lie.

August 11, 1999 was a day everybody in Germany had been waiting for. The last total solar eclipse had happened in 1961 – whole generations, mine included, had never experienced one. "SoFi", as the event of "Sonnenfinsternis" (i.e. "dark sun") was abbreviated affectionately, was the cause for parties that had been planned a year ahead. Some people even booked solar eclipse flights. The entire German market was sold out of eclipse glasses. But I had managed to purchase some.

I clocked out of my office at noon. Along with my colleagues, I walked to a nearby open field where we stood watching the sky. A thickly clouded sky. It got duskier by the minute. Street lamps and neon signs on commercial buildings sprang on. The birds stopped singing, dogs started howling. And then the skies broke open, and instead of my solar eclipse glasses I was very much in need of my umbrella. I never saw the sun at 12:32 pm that remarkable day. It was totally eclipsed by fat, dark, low-hanging clouds.

Almost 20 years later, I've had my second chance to watch a total solar eclipse on August 21, 2017. This time half a world away. My husband and I decided to make it real special.

We didn't want the "only 94 percent" eclipse in Olympia. We wanted to get the entire 100 percent down at the coast in Oregon. We were even contemplating to go camping there just to be in time for the watching. But, of course, camping sites were all booked way ahead of time, and hotel room prices sky-rocketed from between 400 dollars near Long Beach, WA, up to 1,000 dollars near Portland, OR, months before the eclipse. Through some infinite stroke of luck, I was able to find a decent motel room at an almost bizarrely normal rate in Astoria, Oregon, only a week ahead.

We set off way early the day before the eclipse, anticipating terrible traffic. The scenic route we had chosen took us to our motel destination in a smooth 3-hour-ride. Sunny summer Astoria was crowded with people, as they had a Farmers Market going, a huge river boat had landed, and quite a few people like us were spending their time there until the eclipse. At an hourly rate we checked the weather forecast. We needed to make a decision. It was not easy, but once we had given each other a quiet nod, we resumed our program even more relaxed.

The day of the total solar eclipse was here. We rose at six and had breakfast on the boardwalk, while watching the busy quiet of the Columbia River. Thick banks of clouds and fog were hovering over the Pacific, moving towards the bar and the mouth of the river to cover the entire coast with a white, impenetrable shroud. Then we headed … north.

We didn't chase for a spot that might not be clouded or foggy in Oregon. We didn't search for a parking lot in an over-crowded area. We didn't wait it out till the last of the observers would have headed homeward so we could have a smooth ride.

Instead, we found a sunny, quiet spot outside a cozy hamlet somewhere in the middle of nowhere in Washington. We had some tailgate snacks. We watched the eclipse as the moon started slipping into the sun until it left only a fiery circle segment that traveled clockwise. We listened to the birds singing the first of their two evening songs that day. We watched the twilight with the planet high up in the sky. We felt the air getting chillier. We listened to the silence. We were alone and stunned.

I don't know whether we will ever have another chance of catching a total solar eclipse. But it doesn't seem to be that important either. We made memories that day, just the two of us. And insofar my solar eclipse was total. Maybe a 100 percent would even have been too much. Because sometimes a mere 97 percent is all you need, and less is often a lot more.

Mission Irma

My husband and I had planned to fly out to Florida to help set up hurricane protection for a family member of ours in September. We didn't make it in time. Hurricane Irma beat us by half a week. It didn't change our will to go. It made us even more adamant about our mission.

Let's compare hurricane experiences in my mother country, Germany, and over here. Whereas here we know that hurricane season is over the Atlantic from September through November, there is no such thing in Germany. Over there they come when they come. We call our gales "Orkane" (note the etymological relation to the French word "ouragan"); and they are not subtropical and loaded with seawater, but goaded by a wild mix of high and low pressure areas, wreaking havoc just as much. I experienced my first devastating hurricane in Germany on Boxing Day in 1999. "Lothar" was a quick one that already had killed scores of people in France, before it rushed across Germany. Within five hours it ripped up everything in its way. I remember holding on to a closed window that was throbbing with the gusts, while a sound like breaking matches accompanied the shredding of a forest at the horizon. By the end of the day, that hilltop was bare.

Irma, German TV viewers were told, was almost the size of Germany, and whereas there has never been any hurricane evacuation in Germany, as far as I know, we are all aware of the evacuation of almost the entire coastal stretch of Florida, from the Keys to the Panhandle. Our emergency preparations therefore were quite serious, not knowing what we would run into: medical aid, water cleansing gear, emergency rations – we packed it all. Our airline waived the fee for changing the date of our flight out.

It was a subdued crowd of passengers waiting at SeaTac airport for the non-stop flight to Orlando. Only very few people seemed to be traveling for Disney World. The purser onboard had a tough time making seating arrangements for a family with three tiny kids, at first. And that's when I found solidarity flooding through the cabin suddenly. Passengers volunteered to change seats until all the kids were happily settled near their mother and also the bigger passengers who had swapped found themselves in comfortable non-middle-seats. An after-Irma-effect?

Once we had reached Orlando, it was hard to find our car rental – every single bill board and advertisement was shredded. Utility crews were everywhere, taking care of ripped cables, torn metal poles, and destroyed business fronts.

It turned out to be kind of a pocket of destruction though. Further down south, apart from leafless trees and flooded fields, you wouldn't have been aware of anything different from other times. Except that the turnpike was toll-free. And torn bill board canvas was flapping on unilluminated roadside structures. Once on the Treasure Coast, we ran into more damage again. The saltwater transported by the gales had turned what was left of tree foliage a reddish brown. Boats had slammed into the remnants of docks, been hurled onto shore, or sunk to the tips of their masts. Piles of yard debris as high as five or six foot were sitting by every driveway. A lot of houses were still shuttered. Paint had been razed off, store canopies were in an interim state of destruction and repair. But most of the residential buildings were still standing, unruffled due to their hurricane roofs and sturdy construction.

One of our last days, in the aftermath of hurricane José and before Maria, found my husband and me, after all our chores were finished, at my favorite place out there, Gilbert's Bar House of Refuge on Hutchinson Island. It is a weather-beaten complex of three houses built in the 1890s on top of a reef. The beaches around had mostly been devoured by the recent incessant wild surf. Where a couple of years ago people had lazed it with relax chairs on slightly inclining sandy beaches, seaweed was piled high on steeply climbing remnants of what once used to be. Beach houses were precariously balancing themselves on stilt pilings. And the surf crashing against the reef itself flew up to 15 feet, towering and breaking over anybody standing in the wrong place. Who knows how long the beach houses will withstand hurricanes in the future? Even the slightly battered House of Refuge?

On our way back to the airport, something struck my eye: the only bill board intact on the entire I-95. It thanked the people who had come down to help in Florida. It was humbling. It made me think that, so far, I have always been able to return to a safe and sound home. It has become much less of a matter of course to me now. There are people who are way less lucky,

63

but more resilient than I. And they are still on their Mission Irma, cleaning up and helping each other, while I am having a cup of coffee, writing this.

First Snow

As long as I can remember, winter and snow have almost been synonymous for me. I grew up in Southern Germany, and we always experienced the white load sooner or later. We built snowmen and igloos, went tobogganing down any slope we could find, had snowball fights, ate icicles, and simply enjoyed the sight of snow falling in the beams of early streetlights. The first snow never failed to make me feel enchanted and hope for more. Feathery light, it settles on the ground and fills the air with a crisp smelling blur of whiteness.

The first year I arrived here, I was totally disappointed to hear that the lowlands of Western Washington as good as never see any snow. A winter without snow?! Only in the mountains? Well, I guessed I would be able to deal with it. Trying to see the practical side of snowless winters, I was even beginning to like the thought of it. But then on First Advent that year, while my husband and I were enjoying a beautiful walk through the unique fallow-land of Nisqually Reach, it suddenly was upon us. It started with a few, almost countable flakes, shaped intricately and staying on my coat sleeve. And then it really started coming down. By the time we had reached home (which then was in Steilacoom), the ground was covered by a half-inch of snow. It didn't last, of course, but it was enough to give me that Christmassy childhood feeling.

Last week Friday, the news reported a solid 14 inches of first snow in the Cascades. My husband suggested to go and have a look at Mount Rainier that weekend. I didn't expect to be able to get fully around the mountain. In past years, we never made it to Chinook Pass when coming from the North. We usually had to turn around, as snowplows made it clear that the situation was severe winter weather further up. But last Saturday we made it – all the way from Greenwater across Chinook Pass and through Stevens Canyon up to Paradise. It was a breathtaking world of bright golden and flaming red foliage contrasted by the dark green of coniferous forest, craggy, steep rock faces, and … snow. I couldn't help it and snapped photo after photo. My first snow this year melded fall with the up-coming winter in simply stunning ways.

First snow, yet, is also literally a first experience for many people we see in the mountains these days. Not everybody grows up with the experience of snow. These days, we see entire families from other continents travel up Mt. Rainier and marvel at what is snow. They park in picturesque and not so picturesque spots to take selfies and group pictures in the snow. Often enough, their shoes are not snow-worthy, and they slide and glide through the white matter, laughing loudly, tumbling, getting a grip, finding the experience hilarious and utter fun. Once they have discovered what physical opportunities snow offers, they find plastic bags to slide on and frolic in the snow, children and grown-ups alike. It's wonderful to watch that lightheartedness and joy about something that is taken for granted by so many.

But it's not only people from other continents who experience snow for the first time when they come to the

Cascades. We also drove past a car from Texas last Saturday, parked in the middle of the road. A family of three had walked to the roadside snow that was – in that place – approximately knee-deep. While the father stood looking on, the teenagers went right in and dug their hands into the white fluffiness. Then, the girl turned around, and I thought I noticed a solemn look of wonder on her face. As if she had just experienced snow for the very first time. They vanished in our back window after a moment, and I only hope, that this reverent look was soon replaced by joyful laughter and the same frolicking that I have seen with other people.

When we reached Paradise, the road through Paradise Valley was already closed, barred by hip-high snow. This has only been the first of snow in the mountains this season. Soon, there will be way more, and the passes will be closed again. The mountain world will return to wintry tranquility.

Backyard Visitors

Last May, a few blocks away from where we live, a black bear was treed and removed by the Lakewood police and fire department. I was at home and had no clue that the giant animal had waddled down one main road after another without interception. Funny enough, it worried me less afterwards than what havoc humans wreak around town sometimes. Rather, I felt sorry for the bewildered beast that was restored to the wild and probably never realized what had happened to it.

Whether in our former small-town on the Sound or here, we have our share of daily wildlife visitors, for sure. Not bears usually though. I saw a coyote of an evening back in my first year after my arrival. And ever since, I've been aware that I've never gotten anywhere as near wildlife as here.

I used to live in a suburb of the Southern German city of Stuttgart with its almost 600,000 inhabitants. It is a busy region with lots of "clean" industry, i.e. no smoking chimneys or other major pollution problems anywhere near, but lots of traffic. Yet, Nature is lurking through each and everywhere, with vineyards growing from the tops of the hills right into the middle of downtown, huge forests surrounding the city, and rivers and lakes creating a neat background for recreation.

But wildlife in our suburban backyard was rather smallish, unspectacular animals. I never had any encounter with red deer or boars that were roaming the woods some miles further away. But we had little titmice in the trees and rabbits in the fields. Sometimes, woodpeckers flew into the balcony of

68

my parents' apartment to explore the walls for insects. Sometimes we had little red squirrels chase each other up the trees or around the playground in front of the house. And during warm summer nights, when I kept my bedroom window tilted (a typical German window feature, by the way), I could hear hedgehogs munch away in the grass.

My husband had prepared me to expect "Ricky Raccoon" in our backyard. And indeed, we've had our share of raccoon families. One couple brought all of their four cubs one fall and proudly presented them. One of the little raccoons discovered the rope swing our landlord had left in one of our huge oak trees. It swung there for the better part of an hour. That was in our second Lakewood year. Last summer, in the middle of the day, a lonely, fat raccoon strolled into the garden and made for the swing. I could swear it was that little buddy of yore, whose now heavy body made it hard for him to get up all the way. He never came to the door to beg. He just enjoyed the swing.

The first American bird I got acquainted with were those gorgeous blue Steller's jays. With that funny tuft on their heads, their intelligent eyes, asking for nuts with a harsh cry, but a flirtatiously tilted head, they stole my heart immediately. In our first home, we had four coming on a regular basis. I was able to distinguish them all from each other by their looks and behavior.

Little emerald green and mud brown frogs leapt around our Steilacoom garden pond. Turquoise humming birds flew busily in the front yard trees. Here in Lakewood, we spot a white opossum in our garden every once in a while. And at night we sometimes wake from the rather peculiar smell of a skunk passing through. We feed the birds, and pine squirrels are master beggars and thieves around the feeding stations.

The most amazing invaders of our backyard, though, are always deer. They never fail to astonish us. One year, a family of four became a daily regular, feeding from bushes, then laying down in a sunny spot, chewing the cud. They were well aware of us, but usually they just turned their heads curiously, twirled their ears, then went back to their little chewing routine. In Europe, I'd have thought such animal behavior must be due to a case of rabies. You see deer in deer parks, but not in your garden. Or you spot them from the distance, in rural areas. As soon as they smell you, they will kick up their legs and turn in wild flight.

Out here in Washington State, Wilderness clearly still dominates. Human beings have only borrowed their habitats from Nature. We are living side by side with wild animals. And it is quite an experience to bump almost literally into a deer, while weeding the garden, or while jogging, being eyed by a fawn just on the other side of the road.

National and Nature Parks

As a teenager I laughed when I read in a book by Paul Watzlawick that Americans visiting my mother country allegedly ask whether the Black Forest was open on Sundays. It never occurred to me that it could not be open. Or that people might expect to have to pay an entrance fee or have an annual pass for it. Germany has its National and Nature Parks as well as Bio-spherical Reservations, but they work a bit differently from what Americans are used to from their National and State Parks.

By now you have probably guessed why. Germany is a lot smaller and has been densely settled for thousands of years, way before the concept of Nature or National Parks evolved. Germany's oldest Nature Park is the Luneburg Heath, constituted in 1921. The largest is the Southern Black Forest, which also is part of the National Park Black Forest. A quarter of Germany is dedicated to Nature Parks. But ... they are all sprinkled with settlements through and through. The concept has been built around what hamlets, villages, and towns were there already.

Therefore, when you visit e.g. the Luneburg Heath, you will find areas of the typical mix of sandy and peaty landscape, firs, lakes and heath, dolmen tombs from ages of yore, and, above all, quiet that permeates everything. But not all too far from these areas kept for hikers and maybe bikers – none of whom are permitted to leave the paths (these are sometimes even wired off at ankle height) – you will run into human settlements. A bee keeper's home here, a sheep farm there, a hamlet with a friendly Gasthof (pronounce "gust-hof", i.e. guest court), i.e. rustic restaurant, maybe even a carriage service for those who like to experience the landscape in a more convenient fashion. And then there are gorgeous towns, above all Luneburg, Soltau, and Celle, each with their own amazing history, architectural jewels, and cultural offers. So, is a German National Park or a German Nature Park open on a Sunday or during winter? You bet.

The other way round, an uninformed German tourist arriving in Washington State in late fall with the wish to visit the summit of Mt. Rainier would run into some interesting facts specifically American. The highest location of a ranger station cum lodge and restaurant is way beneath the summit in Paradise, and the summit can only be reached by some Mt. Everest style climbing. In Germany, there would be quite a few alpine cottages every winded mile further up, with restaurants and maybe even rustic overnight facilities. Here, you pay a fee for getting into the National Park. And the National Park is not always accessible or only to some point, especially when it has been snowing. Areas without cell phone connections? Here it is a given, over there it is unknown.

So, which of the two concepts do I prefer? I have to admit that I have no preference. I love remembering hikes in the German Alps or in the Black Forest, ending up for lunch at one of the afore-mentioned cottages on an alpine meadow or in a quaint village. I also love the immensity of almost inaccessible primeval landscape and being all by yourself, just meeting very few other hikers in places. I love the concept of integrating human settlement into protected nature. But I also love stepping into protected nature as if it were a separate room, a sanctuary, with the park entrance as its door. I love the loop trails that my mother country provides seemingly everywhere – you never walk back the same trail, but still end up where you started from, on safe paths with bridges and railings. I like the concept of hikers being just guests, too, and Nature showing you her strength in washing out a path, ripping away a bridge, and suddenly you are forced to either rethink or return. German National Parks are tame compared to the American wilderness.

I am looking forward to hiking with my husband this summer and fall again. Only recently we bought a book with suggestions for interesting tours all around Western Washington, some of the quality of a leisurely saunter, some quite challenging. Hiking books – I grew up on them, and I'm happy to find them around here as well. So, let's strap our rucksacks, tie our boots, grab our sticks, and head out to the great outdoors! And let's return refreshed and with a new set of memories made by Nature. Wait – did we renew our Discovery Pass already?

Rivers

Have you ever enjoyed a river cruise? Or any kind of boating trip on a river? On a riverboat? Tell me I'm wrong, but here in Western Washington the only navigable river as in riverboats and freight ships is the Columbia river. The rest of them are barely useable for even small watercraft. It was a difference that only slowly dawned on me. I come from a country with quite a few navigable rivers.

My hometown, Stuttgart, has a sizeable freight harbor and quite a few passenger ships that travel up and down the river Neckar. The river is approximately 225 miles long, of which 126 miles are navigable. There is only a short navigable stretch of it upstream. But between Stuttgart and Mannheim the river rolls on and on past vineyards, small-towns, castles, and low mountain ranges until it reaches the river Rhine. A total of 27 locks helps ships over the long descent of the river Neckar. There are power plants all along the river, too. The downside of creating such a navigable and economically useful waterway is that over the centuries it has lost all of its natural cause inside the navigable stretch.

There are the river Elbe, the Danube, the Oder, Moselle, and the river Main – just to name the most popular and well-known ones; all of them are navigable. And then, of course, there is the river Rhine. It springs in the Swiss Alps, reaches and travels through Lake Constance, creates its mighty falls between Switzerland and Germany at the small-town of Schaffhausen, and becomes all majestic and navigable from

Basel to its North Sea reach in the Netherlands. There are freight barges traveling between Basel and Rotterdam, but also ever so many cruise ships transporting tourists from all over the world. Downstream the trip goes past the Black Forest and the vineyards of France's Alsace, through those of the Palatinate, into the legendary Rhine gorge with its castles and fortress ruins, the Lorelei rock and turreted islands, past the mighty cathedral of Cologne and Europe's largest inner harbor, Duisburg, growing wider and wider until it crosses the Dutch border.

This year, Germany has experienced an extreme drought. Only a couple of weeks ago I read about an island that has suddenly popped up in Lake Constance. As the water level was sinking, sediments at the river Rhine mouth simply accumulated instead of being washed away. Further down the river, near Mainz, car ferries were hardly able to navigate with barely a few inches under their bottom. Cruise ships had to stay anchored, and buses transferred the tourists to the sights they'd otherwise have seen from aboard a riverboat. Sandbanks have emerged where usually ships pass over. Beaches have turned even wider and created quite a Mediterranean ambience to bathing vacationers all summer long until late in September. Yes, there are swimming areas all along the river Rhine, too.

What strikes me as most different between American rivers and their German counterparts? German rivers are used touristy more often and more diversely so. That includes boardwalks along the riversides with restaurant terraces on the water and plazas with benches for flaneurs. There are river walks and local boat lenders galore. There are firework events on the rivers and boating parades. There are historical boat competitions and historical boat tours. Some of the boat services can even be used like a bus – those on the river Neckar bring you from town to town.

Here in Western Washington, rivers still enjoy their natural beauty in most places. It keeps them unrulier for sure, but it also keeps Nature around intact. Except for the Ballard locks and those in the Columbia river, I wouldn't know of further such installations. None that would have the purpose to make a waterway navigable, that is. Not that it makes me homesick. But every once in a while, a little river restaurant terrace … ah, I leave it to your imagination.

Just Pondering

November Moods

Ask Germans to name the bleakest month of the year, and you will probably end up with a unanimous vote for ... November. It's as if the year, once a balloon, had lost all its air and remains but a floppy rubber bladder that stretches, but holds nothing. November – an accumulation of fog, drizzle, rain, cold weather, late dawns, and early dusks.

It doesn't help that it starts with All Hallows', a quite solemn church holiday, and that it pretty much ends with a Sunday commemorating the dead. The Sunday before, Germany has its Memorial Day with church and secular gatherings in most of its cemeteries. As a rookie journalist, I had to cover a bunch of those for our local newspaper. TV broadcasts about the German Memorial Day, or Volkstrauertag (pronounce: fohlx-trower-tuhk, literally: people's grieving day), usually with politicians laying wreaths at central monuments. We remember all the fallen German military, no matter what cause they fought for, but because they died before their time and left behind family. We don't have a Veterans' Day – our fairly recent history makes us tiptoe around any current military issues.

So, is November in Germany such a dreary affair? Actually, the stores will be decorated for Christmas same as over here. You would even recognize lots of the music on their continuous loops. Of course, we lack such a wonderful family fest (or should I say feast?) such as American Thanksgiving. We do have ours, a church Sunday, right after the September harvests – not commemorating any specific event, but another harvest that could be reaped. No turkey meals with specific sides, no housewives laboring to exhaustion over creating and serving fancy dish after dish, while the rest of the family enjoys Thanksgiving football. (And still, isn't everybody looking forward to this opening to the Christmas season, year after year, again and again?!)

While we are thanking and honoring our veterans for all their sacrifices for the nation over here on November 11, Germany actually has two totally different events happening on the same date. The first is the beginning of the so-called fifth season. So, if you have to make a business call (or any call at all) to the German Rhineland on November 11 – better defer it to the day after. Carnival season opens, for whatever reason, on 11/11 at 11:11 am with parades, street celebrations, costumes, and confetti. All offices are closed, though it is no bank holiday, and if you live in the Rhineland, you better go along with it.

For German Catholics, November 11 is also observed as St. Martin's Day. There are Martin's geese for dinner. And children all over the country (not just Catholic ones) can't wait till dusk when people meet at local churches, kindergartens, or schools to go for a lantern walk. We used to craft our own lanterns, and our generation's children are crafting them again. I don't know whether the lantern walkers prefer LEDs these days, as they are considered safer. When I was a child, we had real candles in those lanterns, and some spare ones in our pockets. I will never forget the flickering of a match in the cold

November evening air, the lighting of the wick, the first whiff of melting wax, or the wavering of the flame that shone through the decorated paper lanterns. As candle after candle was lit, we started singing lantern songs, and the millipede of a St. Martin's procession wove through as many neighborhood streets as possible.

November is only as bleak as you make it yourself, I think. It's a month that gives us a break from a busy summer. It has gotten families with school children used to a new school year routine. We can lean back and look across the year and still look forward to some more weeks to come. All leisurely. We should embrace the quiet this darker and less colorful month holds for us and take the time to reflect about ourselves instead of what needs to be done next...

Okay, I'm not true to my own recommendation here. Because I'm planning ahead already. I'm looking forward to celebrate Thanksgiving with my husband at our cozy home. With all the fancy flounces and frills. Adieu, Tristesse!

Train of Thoughts

Trains have something nostalgic about them. So do train rides – not so much those for the sake of commuting to work in suburban areas as those undertaken for leisure. Maybe it is because their pace is so steady and calm. Maybe it is the landscape you pass through and wouldn't see from any car window. Maybe it is because you need a vehicle to get to the station and another one to get away from your destination. Maybe it is even a certain charm of the inconvenient.

Trains to me have been a mode of vacation transportation in Germany for a long time. My first one as a three-year-old went to a tiny seaside resort on the Baltic Sea. It was a night train, and I'll never forget the bustling main station in Stuttgart where we started our trip after a cab had dropped us off. I was way too excited to sleep in my bunk-bed in our family compartment. I watched the moon float above fields and forests it softly illuminated. And at some stations it hung over the roofs of houses that had closed their shutters as if they were tired eye lids.

Later, in my early twenties, I traveled across the Hindenburg Dam to the North Sea island of Sylt. What a strange feeling to see the waves lapping against the foundation over which your train crosses, while you are somewhat tense and just want to reach terra firma again. And there is that tiny old train from the late 1800s on the island of Borkum. Germany's last emperor used to travel in one of its cars from the harbor to his residence. It was all wooden with lead glass windows, a bit like

82

the Rainier train, and it steamed through the languid landscape of dunes and salt meadows.

The last time I traveled a train in Germany for leisure was in 2013 with my husband. I had deliberately chosen a slower train instead of a high-speed ICE especially for the stretch that lies between the cities of Cologne and Mainz, the Rhine Gorge. I remember traveling it ever so often, passing the steepest vineyards you can imagine, traversing cozy small-towns with fancy villas and gorgeous wineries, inviting restaurants on the waterfront, castles and ruins on almost every hilltop. Barges were traveling the river, and pleasure boats almost made you wish to interrupt the journey and hop on. I wanted my husband to experience this wonderful piece of anciently grown cultural landscape.

Reality looked very different, alas. Our train entered the gorge alright, and it stopped at one station I remembered well from past travels. But then it continued and ... wait, wait, wait! It went all into the wrong direction! For it climbed the heights of the Rhine Gorge and from there, no view of the river anymore, went through a none-descript mix of fields, fallow land, and industrial parks. The stops were long. The vistas were those of DIY markets and advertising boards instead of glimpses into the busy everyday-life of a river town. I could have cried. We might just as well have taken the faster train and have been done with the trip more quickly. Here was a piece of my traveling history passed forever into the abyss of fond, un-relivable memories.

Only recently, The Suburban Times published an article that one of the most beautiful stretches of passenger trains in Western Washington would soon be traveled no more. So, my husband and I decided we must take the chance and board a passenger train from Tacoma to Olympia at least once before that was going to happen. It was an interesting find that seating is assigned by the conductors and not electronically, and that their handwritten stubs were crammed into a crevice above the seats instead of the use of a digital board as on German trains. Foot space was incredibly generous, even in coach class. And then the train started moving and went past Ruston Way, popped out of a tunnel near Salmon Beach, and passed the Narrows Bridge and Titlow Beach. You could see Day Island from its normally invisible backside, went across one of America's last vertical-lift bridges across Chambers Bay, past Steilacoom, through Cormorant Passage with a gorgeous fall vista of Ketron Island, and traveled all the way down to the ship wreck in the Nisqually Reach where the train tracks turn land inward. Our trip ended in the middle of nowhere, at Centennial Station in Olympia-Lacey, a pretty little place with a bus stop and a working old-fashioned telephone.

A few hours later, we were on our way back. The snowy Olympic Mountains were out on the other side of the Sound. It may have been one of the best traveling days for this unique stretch of train tracks. People were standing in the aisles, aiming their cameras and smart phones at the windows. I must have taken more pictures that day than I would have any other day without the knowledge I was here for my first and last time.

I won't discuss the policies of railroad companies here, as the decision to run only freight trains along the shores of Puget Sound in the future is a fait accompli anyhow. I won't discuss that freight doesn't care about vistas, but passengers do. I will console myself with the thought that at least these lonesome people at the front of trains with sometimes more than a hundred freight cars will be able to see this incredible piece of landscape on their endless journey. And I will wave to them as they pass us maybe under a bridge or while we are boating.

Tranquility

Are you feeling stressed out about running your Christmas errands (and doesn't the verb "running" already describe the reason so well?!)? About stressed-out people taking it out on others with road rage or nagging in long supermarket lines? Are you hoping to just get the holidays over and done with? Though you really love them and are looking forward to them each and every year anew? Then, maybe, you should step back a little from what you are doing now, breathe deeply, and get yourself a little break.

Maybe, you just need to look back on your achievements this year. No, forget about numbers or sizes or prizes. Maybe you look back on the people you made smile. On the people you gave some love. Or whom you didn't even like, but made an effort for. Look back at what made *you* smile. I am almost willing to bet these were all things you wouldn't have been able to buy or to compete about.

Who really cares how big your Christmas tree is (or even if you have one)? It is you who is going to celebrate with or without it. Whose business is it how heavy your turkey or ham is and how many sides you make? Stress less about it – most of us have way more than enough on their tables anyhow. Rather than think of all the things you ought to do with the left-overs … make less from the start. Who says that it has to be ham or turkey anyhow? You are the one making and eating it. And everyone at your table will be happy about a meal to enjoy together. Who cares how big, how many, or how expensive your Christmas gifts are going to be? Set yourselves a limit. You don't have to go into debt because a jeweler offers you their friendship. You don't have to rush after every fad just because your friends tell you that you have to have this and that (I have had enough of such in my past, thank you!).

So, sit back and reflect what you wish most for during your holidays. Then make yourself a list of what you really need to do in order to achieve this. Then have a piece of chocolate or a cracker with cheese. Breathe! Life is only as stressful as we let ourselves make it. And a lot of the holiday stress is home-made, believe me.

Another wonderful remedy against stress is – a walk. Again: Stop thinking competition. It doesn't matter how long or how fast, as long as you do it for yourself. Leave your smart phone at home; the world will keep on turning without it, and you don't need to be available 24/7. Don't most of us remember when phones were screwed to the wall? We made outings and traveled without carry-around phones, and nobody was the worse for it either side of the line.

Leave your MP3 player a home. Enjoy the silence. Or rather: Enjoy the sounds of Nature. Can you discern birds by their call? Is there a brook murmuring somewhere in the woods? Hear the lapping of the waves against the shore? Is this children's laughter? Do you hear the wind whisper in the branches of the mighty trees around here?

Breathe in deeply and smell. This time of year, the air is tangy with the decay of leaves and fruit, but also spicy with the fragrance of evergreens and rain. It clears your nose. It chills your cheeks. Maybe you started out walking with your hands in your coat pockets or gloved, and by now you are warm enough to move your hands freely.

Enjoy the colors of winter – the reds and yellows of some left-over leaves in trees, the shape of cattails in the swampier parts of this lake, the shiny white berries in that bush over there. How your path is curving through the underbrush. How the lake ripples where a duck just dove...

Excuses not to walk are made easily. And I know them too well. It's cold and rainy outside? Bundle up, take an umbrella. If there are no people around, the greater the tranquility. You've got no time? Ah, think of all the hours you are spending twittering or being on Facebook, about watching meaningless soaps or just flipping through TV channels. Take part of that and turn it into a walk. By the time you are in the middle of it, I promise you that a sense of pride and balance will begin to spread in you. You are doing something for yourself. You have the time to be with yourself, clear your plans, reflect your strategies.

I have found the bleakest, rainiest days here in Washington often the most rewarding ones for a walk. When the vapor over Waughop Lake rises and the ducks huddle in the reeds. When the first snowflakes whirl over the barren land of the Nisqually Reach. When fog envelopes the islands between Chambers Bay and the other side of the Sound. Coming back, all refreshed, I find that my values have been reset to "normal" again and that I *do* have time and tranquility for my Christmas preparations after all. I just need to kick my shins harder to step outside my door more often.

Naming Objects

Have you ever hesitated to call anything you know by its real name? Not as in knowing its name and just not coming up with it for a second – but as in not knowing it at all? It is even stranger to recognize what you see and to know its name in your mother tongue, but not in the foreign language that you use every day. Or even not to know what you are seeing and trying to find its correct name. That is what linguistically different immigrants deal with on a constant basis in their chosen new home country.

It can be hilarious, especially for those people who are not aware that even a fairly fluent speaker as I runs into such a ditch every once in a while. Often enough, it's that I recognize the word as soon as somebody else gives it to the object whose name I have been looking for. You call that passive language skills, and every avid reader probably has an abundance of this. My English is a strange mix of British and American words – which probably accounts for bewildering quite a few people once I open my mouth or let my fingers type my thoughts.

One case that I remember especially vividly happened in the early fall of 2012. My husband still teases me about it every once in a while. We were gardening together, and I desperately needed an implement that he had used before, but was nowhere to be seen around anymore. I racked my brain, and finally came up with a solution. Description of an object's looks sometimes helps another person fathom what you mean. So, I asked my husband for the "garden fork" (not knowing that there is, indeed, a tool that goes by this name). As we were about to see to fallen leaves, he quickly grasped that I meant a "rake". It's certainly not the only term that I had stowed away somewhere in my brain, but that didn't want to come to my tongue that day in this foreign language.

Another case involves a cute furry animal from the Mt. Rainier area that I discovered one summer day in my very first year here. How frustrating to know what I was seeing – a "Murmeltier" (pronounce 'moor-ml-teer) – but not the name it went by in English. My husband told me its name, and, for the rest of that summer, I kept messing it up with the brand of a British food item of quite similar pronunciation. May the marmot forgive me.

What strikes me as even more disturbing to this day is my ignorance about a lot of natural beings which I cannot name simply because I don't even know what they are. And it's a tough one to find out about every single one of them. One of my first Washington summer mornings, I looked out onto our patio and suddenly saw something bright blue alight and vanish. Something bright blue that doesn't occur in more subtly colored Germany. It took me days to figure what the bird looked like in detail, as it was quite shy at first. Then I started to google. "Blue bird, black tuft" or something similar ended me up with an appropriate "Steller's jay". It was way more difficult to find the name for another blue bird without the tuft, the "Californian thrush jay". You get the picture.

I was pretty good at naming animals and plants in Germany. My grandmother and my mother had made it a given that, wherever we went, we children were taught the identifying clues to discern trees, flowers, bushes, birds … As a child I found it incredibly tedious. But today I'm grateful that they somehow made me listen and learn after all.

Speaking English as a foreign language means to be detached from the natural implicitness native speakers are used to – naming those natural objects that are inherent here. An Alaskan friend of mine taught me what a salmonberry looks like. A gardening one told me the name for German "Schachtelhalm" (pronounce 'shuh-tl-hulm), that I very vaguely remembered from the Black Forest and which grew in abundance in the yard of our first home over here – horsetail. A befriended couple was aware of my deep frustration of not knowing birds of the Pacific Northwest and even sent me a book on ornithology – finally I know the names of Northern flickers, chickadees, robins, or red breasted nuthatches at our backyard feeder. My husband added further books on birds and plants in the region. I am doing my best to learn about whatever I discover here. But there is no doubt that in some aspects I will always stay an immigrant from another part of this world.

National Anthems

I hail from a country that, for a long time, had lost any national pride at all due to its horrible history. We have lost permission to sing our national anthem's first stanza, because during the Third Reich it was seen as a justification to conquer land, not as a call to unify many states into one nation. Pretty much every German soccer fan knows the third stanza, which is our anthem's text now, by heart. It hasn't been always like this. And we hear the anthem quite rarely, too.

The German national anthem is played only on official occasions involving international context. It is, as far as I know, never heard at an inner-German sports event. Other European nations deal with their anthem in the same way. So different from what we know about the Star-Spangled Banner. Basically, it is to discern the competitors of different nations on whatever occasion. Until the 80s, you often saw the national German soccer team on the lawn, standing bored and slack, chewing gum, spitting, or even talking to each other, while the national anthem was playing. It all changed with a new coach, Franz Beckenbauer, former soccer top-star, who brought elegance and style to the stadiums again. Not only was he the trendsetter for coaches to wear suits and ties on the bench, he made it obligatory for the entire team to sing the national anthem. The stance of the men changed entirely. These days, those young men are singing the anthem with fervor and sometimes with tears in their eyes, and the entire German fan block sings along.

By heart. And then … no applause. Because you don't applaud something as sacred as an anthem.

Only recently, after a particularly badly botched US anthem at a basketball game, I happened to listen to a top ten of worst performed US anthems in sports history. And I was appalled. Maybe, I'm having an Andy Rooney moment here, so please forgive me my ranting. There are apologies out there for every singer who didn't deliver. Some say they were so nervous. Others say maybe it was the flu. Or they couldn't read the wording they had penned into the sweaty palm of their hands. Seriously?

The Star-Spangled Banner tells a story. It's descriptive. It's painting a vivid image. And somebody is not able to remember the wording of an anthem that has been played so often, that they should know it just by hearing? I mean, these are professional singers up there. They are singing in their mother tongue. They remember all the songs they have ever written or performed for their own fame. But not the US anthem?

The top ten of worst renditions of our anthem made me deeply pensive. It almost seems like these days all those stars are out to show off themselves, while performing. The beautifully simple, yet challenging melody that almost sounds like the lonely song of a cornet has obviously become the fairground for performers who find they are better than this. As in who can free-style yodel the best – and, here, yodeling is not derogatory, but the terminus technicus for when the voice

94

moves from one register to another without bracing. Who can keep their breath the longest while singing the words "land of the free"? And who can maybe even reach a quart higher than the original composition at that point? Afterwards, there's a TV discussion about what went wrong where. And it's always about the singer, not the anthem. That is, in my humble opinion, the reason for so many professionals failing to get our anthem right. They have managed to turn singing the anthem into an unofficial competition amongst themselves. About themselves. And the audience claps their performance.

A while ago, I was at a military retirement celebration, and the national anthem was performed by a very young, very nervous lady. As a semi-pro, I know that it takes guts to appear before an audience. She was singing the US anthem for her father, and she sang it heart-felt. She knew her words, and she put meaning into them. She was not pitch-perfect, but she did the anthem honor. This young lady was not a star, but simply real and true. I guess, all of the listeners were touched. That is what our anthem should do to us. That was when, for once, I clapped its singer.

History

A little while ago, I had a wonderful reading event at a yarn store near Lakewood Town Center. I was reading a chapter from one of my novels to a group of lovely, witty, and very sophisticated listeners. That chapter contained the story of one of my novel characters, including a short compilation of German 20th century history. At the end of the session I was asked how much of it I had had to research. I said "none". And then it struck me why.

My life story has been one of hearing family history. My favorite picture books used to be family photo albums. And when my grandmother visited, she always told of her youth, but also of her life during and shortly after World War II. Basically, our family was so much affected by the war that this part of History became part of our family history. True, later on, at school, all the political details were filled in. And Germany was intense about this when I grew up. We heard about the Third Reich in the school subjects of German, history, religious education, art, music, politics. We were doused with facts in documentaries and Hollywood movies. We were aware of it at each and every step, reading explanatory street signs and the inscriptions of monuments. We encountered it traveling into our neighboring countries. My generation is still horrified and deeply ashamed about what a people can let happen.

But history lessons also involved so much more. We studied it from grade 7 through grade 13 at grammar school – and it was fascinating what repetitive patterns were perceivable.

What clever or crooked personalities created boon or bane for their nation. It was a intriguing virtual trip around the world, and today I only wish there had been even more of it and that I had listened so much better. I am still studying history at every chance I get, and I feel it is like time and geographic traveling rolled into one.

When I came over here, the first time I came past such typically Western façades of houses as in the center of Roy or Wilkeson I was dumbfounded. Even more so when entering a pub and finding guys wearing Stetsons and cowboy boots. And then only it hit me. This is part of continued History, too!

I grew up around literature and movies that dealt with the Wild West. I knew about the Oregon trail and was wildly fascinated with it. I secretly envied those adventurous settlers who had dared to push the frontier farther and farther out west to the reaches of Washington Territory. I often thought I would have loved to be part of that. Little did I know that one day I'd actually live here and have to realize that the phantasmagoric stories presented by Western movies happened basically only a bit over 150 years in Western Washington's past.

I might have learned a lot about world history at school, through family history, literature, or movies. But I still have to wrap my head around the fact that only 200 years ago this place was pure wilderness and that only native Americans roamed the prairies, the lakes, and the bays of what once would be named South Puget Sound. That this place developed within record speed from log cabins to high rises, from canoeing as the fastest way of transport to Interstates, from clearing farmland with axes to crop dusters. That some people here are directly connected to those pioneers who settled this country. Meaning: I might have learned world history, but nobody ever gets taught the closer picture about another country.

In fourth grade we were taught Heimatkunde (pronounce: 'high-mutt-coon-dah, meaning local history, geography, and economy). That is what I am reading up on these days – this area's history. That is what I keep learning when being a docent for the Steilacoom Historical Museum. That is what I encounter when meeting friends and talking about their experiences. Of course, they know when certain events in their family's past took place. Of course, they toss around names of people and places. It's because it's been lived history, not just studied history. And, believe me, it's just as intriguing to me when you tell me your history as it might be to you when I tell you mine.

End of Summer

Though, according to the calendar, it will be summer for a few weeks yet, we all know that Labor Day pretty much marks the end of summer everywhere in the United States. Certainly here in Western Washington. In Germany, Labor Day would be in May and mark the beginning of early summer. So much for what holidays are about and what they really mean to people. As to the end of summer, I think people feel pretty much the same about it anywhere.

Here, the ferries will fill with the last of summer people leaving their island residences. The roads will be congested with campers returning home with their RVs. SeaTac airport will be overcrowded with passengers departing for their homes somewhere else in the States or returning from their vacations. And then, one night in your favorite corner pub, you will realize that all of the sudden it's just you and the other local regulars again.

It is also this time of year that some people seem to skip every thought about a gorgeous fall lying in wait with brilliant colors against a bright blue sky or against the first low gray clouds. They announce that it is only that many more weeks till Christmas and seem to justify that supermarkets start turning out Christmas items already and TV broadcasts Christmas movie marathons again. The first farmers markets vanish from sight though there is still so much colorful bounty out there. But I guess, it is the worry about customer frequency during colder and wetter days that reduces their number so very suddenly.

Schools start announcing all kinds of activities on their billboards. School busses that have been parked somewhere invisible all summer long suddenly fill the roads in droves again, and you better be aware that their stopping means that you stop, so kids can safely cross the road. It means that in school zones speed limits are enforced more strictly again. And that, as the mornings are staying darker longer, you better watch the road shoulders in case some little ones are waiting to be picked up by their school bus in the murky dawn.

The end of summer also means that you gather the last of your garden harvest and maybe can it or share it with your neighbors. That the trees in your yard start getting barer, the squirrels in them furrier, and your gutters fill with leaves. It means you switch off your fans and ACs and switch on the lights earlier. The patio furniture might get used a last time on one of the warmer September days. And in the evenings, you hear the Canada geese fly across in formation, their honks sounding like a rusty garden pump, gathering to move further south.

The end of summer has got the blues, no doubt. A very soft one, with the reminiscence of bared skin and ice cream, of watering thirsty garden beds and of dusty country roads, of juicy berries gleaming on bushes and of children's laughter from secret gardens. It carries the seething ache of Nature falling asleep and dying, of colors so vibrant that we know they cannot last. It brings along a sense of isolation and huddling up at home.

End of summer – a last boating tour on the Sound, a farewell to splash parks and fountains, a final hike in the mountains before the first of snow hits the summits.

End of summer – and the year rolls on, every year seemingly faster.

End of summer. But we know there will be another summer next year.

Service Stars

"Service Desert Germany" – unfortunately that is one of the self-bestowed nicknames of my mother country. At least it was true in many ways when I lived there. Who knows where it derived first or whence? I guess it all started when Germany recovered from World War II. At first, pretty much everybody was lending a hand to make survival possible in a totally destroyed country. But with the onset of a healthy economy, with the food wave of the Fifties, and the traveling wave of the Sixties, obviously quite a few people forgot what it means to lend a hand. The first so-called guest-workers were transported into Germany from Italy. Later, there came more from all over the Mediterranean countries. When the Iron Curtain vanished, people from the former Eastern Block states arrived.

Today, a huge chunk of the German gastronomy is in foreign hands. So are small grocery stores and delicatessen, gas stations, dry cleaners, shoe makers, or locksmiths. Utility services such as garbage are mainly operated by immigrants. Trades such as carpentry, construction work, plumbing, or car mechanics are often learned by the children of former immigrants. Whereas Germans either charge more money or offer less service, their businesses rely on traditions in which the family plays a big role – and that enables them to offer good service at lower prices. If anybody complains about so many businesses and services in Germany not being in German hands anymore: the desire for quick money with as little effort as possible is the sad reason.

Arriving in a small-town in Washington and trying to find my way around, made me aware that service is not a question of ethnicity. For my first experiences were with sales assistants in supermarkets, with officials at administrations, and with staff at a military hospital. Let me share it with you.

Doing groceries on my own for the very first time over here, I had to scan aisle after aisle for everything that I needed, of course. It took me long to get to the bottom of my short list, with many detours and returns to a number of aisles. Surely – and don't ask me why – one of the articles I "needed" was anchovies' fillets, and I simply couldn't find them. Not knowing what the product would look like (would it come it in a jar or a can?) didn't make it easier. A sales associate noticed my cluelessness and asked me what I was looking for. I didn't expect her to be much of a help. The most I expected was being sent to another aisle – because that's what usually happens in Germany: "Das ist da hinten" – as in "you'll find it back there". Instead, the sales associate took me to a specific aisle, she also checked the shelves until she found the can I'd been searching for. Ever since I've kept coming back to this supermarket, experiencing the kindest service imaginable. It feels unbelievably comfortable, and I have developed real friendships with quite a few of the service personnel – amongst them that lady who helped me that very first time.

Grumpy officials in administrations? I needed to see Social Security a month after I had arrived over here as my "Green card" hadn't made it in the mail to me. The lady at the

103

window was not only focused on her job, she also seemed to know what worried me. So, she didn't just check her computer about it, but she actually filled in forms with me – and the very next day I had my paperwork in my mailbox. I call that customer-oriented! Service was friendly and impeccable. For sure, German administration employees are also friendly. But they usually don't get to that level of personal communication I found over here in Washington State.

Though I had heard rumors galore about unfriendly staff at a nearby military hospital, I would see for myself when I had to go in for an emergency. Not only was the receptionist very friendly, but also the nurse who took over from there. I bet she didn't earn a fortune, but she gave away a fortune in kindheartedness and emotional support. Later she saw to it that I didn't feel forgotten in the waiting room, but kept coming off and on to see to me. Memories flood back of a time I spent as a youngster in a German civilian hospital. Nurses there left me, a then very shy teenager (too shy to ask for anything) thirsting in my hospital bed for an entire long night, and they almost let me walk with a tube still in my arm. I recall gruff nurses at another German hospital with church connections. It reminds me of German doctors who wouldn't tell you that they were performing minor surgery you until after they were done. In doctors' offices and hospital over here I feel like a person, not like a case that needs to be rushed through. I call that a holistic approach to medicine.

There are countless situations each of us experiences each and every single day around here. If you grew up here, you are probably used to that. I find the level of individual involvement at all kinds of institutions and businesses often exceptional. This high level of service is frequently delivered in places I don't expect it. It's not only provided by ethnic minorities who want to make a living. I find it at all levels of hierarchies and over all ethnicities. And I certainly realize how much of my daily level of feeling good derives from these friendly service encounters.

Vibrance, Flavors, Fragrances

The other day, in a local supermarket, I was standing in the dairy aisle, looking for my usual brand of sour cream. It was clean sold out, so I was checking out different brands. To my utter surprise one of the tubs said "Natural flavor added". You know me by now: I was not only flabbergasted, I was clean disgusted. Why would you need to add natural flavor to a natural product? Unless the product is so bad and bland that you wouldn't want it in the first place?

I have no idea how many naturally flavored products I have eaten in my lifetime. After all, one of the leading manufacturers of natural flavors is near Heidelberg, an hour's drive away from my hometown in Germany. I've never really come to terms with wood chips pretending to be strawberries or mold creating flavors such as peach, nut, or coconut. The older I become the less I think it makes sense, especially since a lot of those flavored products don't taste anywhere near the original flavor experience. And I'm never sure what chemistry I ingest with it. Well, I guess, a lot of the fruity flavors go into candy – that in itself is not health food, right? But do I have to have strawberry-flavored apple juice? Or fake fruit in a yogurt, flavored and dyed to assume the experience you have when eating a strawberry or a blueberry?

Ah, here goes my next favorite topic: food dyes. And I'm pretty sure I never ran into that amount of it in Germany. One thing that really struck me from the first over here was blue icing. I have a feeling there is an extra high rate of blue icing sales here in Washington State. For one, we have the Seahawks (with an additional shade of green to the cake). And as a retired Air Force spouse I've had my share of tongue-coloring blue-iced dessert cakes as well. There are rainbow cake batters and colored sprinkles, and not just kids fall for it. Of course, *they* do! It's the older generations that pack all the dyes into kids' food to make it appear more edible. With the effect that natural produce like vegetable or fruit are less appreciated than colorful cupcakes or candy. I'm not sure we are doing them a favor. Lately I leafed through a recipe book of mine and came across a recipe for deep-frying batter. It called for yellow food dye. Why?!

And then there are fragrances. Scented candles, scented oils, scented potpourris, scented you name-its – you don't even know what's in them. Yes, we do have them in Germany, too. I never was one for them. I love the elegance of white taper candles. I don't want additional smell. My home is filled with the fragrance of cooking and baking. Right now, the tart scent of apples from our neighbors' garden adds to the mix, along with the smell of rotting leaves when I open the doors or windows. It's a lovely, entirely seasonal fragrance. I have a feeling you could tell what season it is by just walking into our home and sniffing – without having fake sea scents (I wonder whether those were bought if they really smelled of rotting pilings, algae, and wet sand), pumpkin latte, or Christmas cookie aromas. Why would I want to mix the delicious smell of a pot roast with the artificial fragrance of "rain", which actually tends to remind me of laundry freshly removed from the washing machine?!

What makes us crave for the artificial when we can have the natural original? It seems to be a human phenomenon. The other day I bought stamps from one of our local post offices. They show those popsicles in incredible color combinations. I wouldn't even want to eat a single one of those if they were for real. I am sure they'd taste as artificial as they look. And – would you believe it?! – when you rub those stamps, they smell!

Pick-Up and Drop-Off

People are talking about how divided this country is, and I see it every day. Not just in a sense of politics – and you know this column was never meant to make any political statements. I find that there is one part of the population who drops off and another who picks up.

Only in October, I came across an invitation by the City of Lakewood to join an event – it was all about cleaning up specific town areas. I always hear how clean everybody finds my native country, Germany. And in a way it's true. It's not necessarily because a lot of Germans didn't drop their garbage wherever they feel like it. It's because we have clean-up crews patrolling parks ,pedestrian zones, and whatnot on a daily basis to pick up the debris other people mindlessly dropped. Paid clean-up crews. As in: It's their job, if not their vocation. This is why I don't remember any volunteers ever cleaning up areas in droves, and certainly not by invite to an "event" either. Because, let's admit it, it's *not* fun to pick up what other people leave behind in their laziness.

Another typical concept over here is the "Adopt a Street" one. You actually pick up the responsibility for an entire street as to picking up litter other people dropped or flung out of their car windows. I mean, really?! You cannot wait until you are parked somewhere to place your garbage into a bin, but you think it proper to toss bottles, garbage bags, and your ashtray contents into the street? Why are some people dropping their trash that they wouldn't drop onto the floors of their private home onto the grounds of our communities?! No, it's not a hen-and-egg problem. Clearly, the drop-off comes before the pick-up.

The phenomenon continues to supermarkets. How often do you find shopping carts dropped off in what seems to be the last available parking slot? I mean, if ever there is laziness, this is it! Because most parking lots have an area where you can drop off your grocery cart – mostly just a few ten yards away from where you have parked your car. I will never forget that well-dressed "lady" coming out of the University Place Safeway's last year around Christmas. It had started to snow. And I'm sure that lady didn't want her outfit to be messed up by the wetness. There was a cart drop-off only about ten yards away from where she had unloaded her groceries into her car. But what did she do? She worked on heaving the front wheels of the grocery cart into a flower bed five yards away in the other direction. Which took her probably as much time and as much effort as if she had dropped it off properly. She obviously never thought of the poor sales associate who wouldn't just have to retrieve all the carts in the drop-off in the cold wetness, but also have to retrieve the cart from the flower bed. How very kindhearted, mindful, and lady-like!

My mother country has long dealt with the phenomenon of grocery carts dropped off anywhere because people are plain too lazy to walk a few more steps. They have invented the deposit cart: You put a coin into a slot in the handle to retrieve a cart – you get it back when you place the cart where the drop-off is by connecting your cart with those already parked. No carts standing around randomly in parking lots, for sure.

I could go on and on about the willfulness of some people. I still wonder about the story behind the wedding cake that friends of mine once found after they had adopted a street and were on their pick-up route. I won't ever understand why people drop trash anywhere. It's absolutely disrespectful not just against the picker-uppers, but against Nature as well. And I think the only places where pick-ups and drop-offs are agreeable is at airports and food banks.

Between the lines

There is a lot of bewilderment for non-native speakers when it comes to talking to Germans in Germany. What should it be? "Du" (pronounce: doo) or "Sie" (pronounce: zee)? When do you use first names and when last names? And when do you say "Frau" (pronounce: frouw, i.e. Mrs.) and when "Fraeulein" (pronounce: froy-line, i.e. Miss)? So much easier in English, right?

Well, it's all a matter of closeness and respect, even in English. Because even though I might call you "Bob" or "Kathy" to your face, when I talk about you in public it will turn into a way more respectful "Bob Last-name" and "Kathy Last-name", if not even into a "Mr. Last-name" and "Mrs. Last-name". And even the "Mrs." might be politically incorrect, depending on how much I know about your marital status. After all, you might be a Ms. Also: Have you ever noticed the slight shift from calling an acquaintance you only just met by their first name to being on first name basis with an old friend? There sure is a difference, right?

As you all know Germans tend to be a bit blunter and more outspoken. It might be this bluntness that lets you know where you are standing with each other. It's definitely a "Sie" combined with "Herr" (pronounce: hair, i.e. Mister) or "Frau" and last names when you have only met a German. By the way, the term "Fraeulein" is totally outdated.

There is that interesting coming-off-age transitional period when teenagers are addressed as "Sie" combined with

112

their first name – a custom that German schools use. Though not a teacher, my mother also stuck to that rule to signal my friends that she regarded them as grown-ups now. I guess it made every one of us grow a few inches as to self-regard. This custom is very similar to when I meet a stranger I'm supposed to call by their first name the first few times we deal with each other. There's that respectful distance between us. Though in English we use the seemingly less respectful "you" all the time.

But here's the deal: Do you know the difference between "you" and "thou"? Apart from running into the terms "thee", "thou", "thy", and "thine" in the Lord's Prayer and other ancient texts? Because actually most Germans think "you" means the same as "du" ... which is not the case. In truth it is way more respectful. Yes, out comes the linguist in me ... "Thou" used to be a very informal and familiar way to address family and friends. Some of you may remember that in Alcott's "Little Women" old-fashioned Professor Baer asks his Jo to address him with "thou" for more familiarity. "Ye" was for addressing several persons, which turns its use for a single person into something way more formal. Over the times and by the 17th century, "thou" was regarded as too disrespectful (and more complex with its conjugational rules, too) and replaced by the more formal "ye", which with vowel shifts and spelling changes became "you". Interesting, isn't it?

So, how do you know a German is your friend? Is it simply in being offered "Bruderschaft" (pronounce: brooder-shuft, meaning brotherhood) in linking arms, while drinking from one's glass, then kissing each other? Most Germans deem this too rustic a tradition. My father has friends whom he has addressed as "Sie" and "Frau" or "Herr" all his lifetime and friends he calls by their first name and addresses as "Du". It's normal. It works for both sides. But this German tradition has softened over the years. And a lot comes from Germany peeping across the fence to the English-speaking nations and misapprehending the combination of using "you" and first names as a more familiar approach when it's all about nuances.

These days, a lot of Germans will tell you: "Say Du, and my first name is ..." There is one hiccup in the process – once you have had a fall-out, it's hard, if not impossible to return to a more distanced "Sie". And it's easier to call someone names once you have allowed for less distance in your relationship by offering to address each other as "Du". Which makes it the perfect mix to call it each other "Sie" on a first name basis.

Did I manage to utterly confuse you now? Ah, languages, the changes they make and the turns they take! And how much lies in a few monosyllabic words to show respect to each other. Even between the lines.

Pastimes

Crabbing

It's over. For most areas in Western Washington, crabbing season this year ended on Labor Day. And though it has its smelly challenges at times, I'll really miss doing it until next year's crabbing marks the summer season again. Which means a lot to come from a city girl who learned how to crab only ever since she moved to the South Puget Sound area.

I wouldn't know that my mother country Germany's North Sea or its Baltic Sea hold any crab at all. If they do, I've never seen any. The only crustaceans I remember are North Sea shrimp: ugly little gray creatures that are tough to peel, but hold immense flavors. There is no recreational shrimping, unless you count going out on a crab cutter with a professional crew. You may watch them sink the net, drag it up again, boil the loot, and then taste one or two. The rest are for sale. Those tours, sold as two-to-three-hour-cruises often with a look at seal colonies, are mostly booked up by city people vacationing by the North Sea and trying to find something authentic. If it is authentic to gawk at a cutter crew hauling shrimp.

Moving to Western Washington, introduced me to recreational crabbing, of course. Every small town on the Sound seems to have their own public fishing dock. With the beginning of crabbing season, which usually coincides with the beginning of June, entire families start flocking to those docks, sometimes equipped with chairs and umbrellas, even full picnic baskets. It can get pretty crammed on these docks, and it becomes almost a friendly kind of competition as to who has already caught how many crabs. One of the most intriguing questions is that about bait – turkey tails, salmon heads, chicken legs, or rather some special item from one of the marinas around? Some people swear by what they are using. So far, my husband and I have been trying out pretty much everything, even rank stuff that would make you shudder, in order to catch crab. Meanwhile, I'm almost sure it's more about location, time of day, and tidal circumstances than what bait you cram into the bait basket inside your trap or net.

These days, during crabbing season, we are rather operating from a small boat. I toss our single trap net overboard when my husband tells me we are at the perfect depth. We check the surroundings for landmarks, so we are sure to find our trap again, and then we head off for some exploring. Usually, coming back from a turn through some quiet bays or from beaching the boat on an island, we immediately check on our trap again. That means that my husband steers the boat near the marker buoy, and I lean overboard to grab it and haul the rope in hand-over-hand and as quickly as possible. More often than not the crabs are too small, and I set them free again. We also agree that we don't want any females, even when legal. In 2016, we didn't catch a single crab of edible size all summer long. In 2017, we were quite lucky.

I would never have believed that I would ever be nimble enough to disentangle live crab from netting without getting nicked by their strong prongs. These beautiful creatures then end up in a wet and iced towel in a cooler and get

118

transported home as soon as we have finished our crabbing trip. Now, here comes the part that is probably the most humbling for a crabber: the coup de grâce. In order to appreciate my food to the full, I wanted to learn to do it myself. A quick, hard blow to the head seems to be more humane than throwing them into boiling water alive. Still, before I kill shellfish, I apologize to them. Hosing out the guts and cleaning the barnacles off with a knife, leaves a carcass that doesn't yield anything disgusting into the steamer on the BBQ. The meat from the body, by the way, is a flaky delicacy, stunning to eat, and easily doubles the amount from the prongs and legs. Have it with clarified butter or turn it into crab cakes – it's a culinary experience. For someone never having dealt with crab before, I think I have adjusted to this part of Western Washington life pretty well.

For whatever reason, we have always only caught red rock crab in our trap, by the way. Not bad either – they are scrumptious. The legendary, sought-after Dungeness crab has managed to elude us, so far. But one has to have a reason to eat out sometimes, too, don't you think?

Traveling

"I would love to travel there!" How often do I hear this after I have just let somebody know that I am from Germany?! Believe me: almost weekly and mostly from people of working age. I never ask why they don't simply do it. I have long realized that there is quite a difference in traveling experiences for Europeans and Americans.

A huge impediment, respectively advantage are distances and traveling times. When I was still living in my original hometown, it took me a mere two hours by car to reach Austria, Switzerland, or France. A two-hour-flight would have brought me all the way into Scandinavia, the United Kingdom, Italy, Poland ... you are getting the picture. Here, in Lakewood, a two-hour drive takes me not even to the eastern state border or the Canadian border and barely to the state border of Oregon. That's how huge Washington State is!

Now let's talk how much vacation time somebody in the United States has compared to a German. It's a no-brainer that with triple the average vacation days, a German can easily spend two weeks on two vacations and then have another two left over for family, emergencies, and other extras. In the US, many people have family in other states. In order to keep in touch, their mere 14 days are spent on family visits, and any leisurely traveling outside the country will have to wait for retirement.

Also, if you want to travel outside the US, it gets very pricey very quickly. The flight outside already is a fortune –

imagine you wanted to do this with a family of four! And then, traveling expenses continue in the country you travel – hotels, food, transportation, souvenirs… Whereas in Europe you can fly with German Wings, Ryan Air, and other airlines on a shoestring budget. Traveling to a destination outside your mother country only gets expensive once you leave Europe.

Quite a few Americans are also scared of traveling outside the US because they don't know foreign languages. Don't worry! These days, almost everybody anywhere in the touristy world speaks English. So, not being understood is definitely not much of an obstacle anymore. But still, to know a foreign language has its clear advantages. For example that of helping to keep budgets down. Travel agencies, stop your ears now! If you know the language of your travel destination, you can book hotel rooms and transport via local websites much more affordably and snatch some charming experiences into the bargain. After all, who wants to stay in an interchangeable national or international chain hotel when they can experience a typical country inn with their regional breakfast buffet?

I have to admit that Germans are at a huge advantage over Americans when it comes to traveling vacation. But though I have had my share of international vacations on four continents and I have always been able to add a touch of vacation to business trips during my time off, I also simply loved to explore my mother country. I have spent extensive vacations on North Sea islands (and still not seen all of them). I have explored the Black Forest and the Bavarian Forest to all their length and width. I have seen pretty much all of Bavaria, from the Alps to the lakes and Franconian beautiful cities and small-towns. I know the Rhine-Ruhr-region well, and have learned to love its industrial charm. The list of my Germany trips is longer – and I still haven't covered so many areas.

So, what can I suggest to a Washingtonian who would love to travel, but doesn't have the money, the courage, or the time?

Start where you live. Take a map of your beautiful state and figure where you haven't been yet. Make a "bucket list". My husband had me write one down when I came here, and it was a Western Washingtonian list only. It was quite a long one. After seven years, we finally have worked it down, and I could triumphantly rip it up only recently. But guess what?! I have already a new one! It is letter-size and Washington State only, line after line after line. It might take us another seven years to see all these places and explore all the areas that I dream of. It will have to happen on weekends when we are not doing work around the house or run other errands. Some trips might include an overnight stay somewhere unknown. There is so much adventure out here!

The Chinese philosopher Lao Tse said that a journey of a thousand miles begins with a single step. It can be taken literally, with a step outside your door and a map in your hands. Drop the GPS, and explore maps again for the places of wonder around you. Traveling can start with a day trip into the unknown. And when you finally have the time to visit foreign countries, you will find you are not just pretty excited about traveling outside your comfort zone. But you will be able to tell people out there how wonderful your home state is.

Gardening

Until I came to the United States, I never had a garden. This is not unusual at all. In comparison to this nation, my mother country, Germany, is tiny, and its almost 90 million inhabitants literally live on top of each other in many places. I grew up in apartment houses. Later I rented apartments without any gardens. I have experienced living at half a stair-flight's level to sixth floor, always with a view of green. But none of these gardens were mine. Unless you call those boxes you can hang from a balcony banister a mini-garden.

I had such boxes. Always. I was never really good at tending to potted plants. I even manage to drown or dry up cacti. The same with boxed plants. But I gave it serious tries. Always. Meanwhile, suburban neighbors with gardens cut roses or harvested zucchini and strawberries, depending on the season. I always consoled myself that they had to mow their lawns and rake leaves, too. So, how much more convenient just to have those small hanging boxes.

It only occurred to me that I would have a garden (if just rented) when I saw the first pictures my husband emailed me after he had moved to the South Sound. I was stunned. It was a property on a steep hill with apple trees and a stonewalled pond; it had flagstone steps and an enormous, partly covered deck. When I arrived almost a year after these first pictures, it was wet and cold with a very late summer beginning only in mid-July. I peered through the windows mostly, huddled in layers of shirts and pullovers, amazed at the rich greens, the

124

brilliant colors of the rhododendrons, the all-conquering brambles and horsetails.

As the year went on, we saw apples grow from tiny hard balls into rich red orbs. I gathered them when they fell to the ground and made the pinkest apple sauce I have ever seen in my life. It was the first time that I was able to reap a harvest from "my" garden. It was incredibly gratifying.

Apart from that, gardening was immensely time-consuming. As soon as I had reached one end of the plot with weeding and cleaning out, I had to return to the other end to start all over again. Fall brought a load of fiery maple leaves onto the sidewalk running outside our rental property – sometimes the town did the cleaning, more often it was us raking and discarding the leaves at a dump.

Winters were quiet and drizzly – our backyard madrone trees with their luscious dark green and the squeaky green lawn at the front of the house gave us a vision of warmer seasons through the dark gray days of the Pacific Northwest. And when the first camellias started blossoming in January, I knew we had made it through to another spring that would shout all the colors of a painter's palette: the gold of daffodils and forsythia, the soft pink shades of Japanese cherry trees, the blues of violets and hyacinths, the abundance of shades in azaleas and tulips.

It is fall again, and we live in another house with another garden in another town. The lawns are flat. We have a circle of nine oak trees (there must have been an entire dozen

125

once) in the back yard. The weather has been lenient so far, and this is one of the first gray and drizzly days, as I'm writing this article. A ray of sunshine makes it through the cloud cover every once in a while, and it enhances the golden foliage from a tree in our neighbor's garden and the garnet red of our Japanese maple in the front yard. Actually, I think the gray October skies create a beautiful backdrop for the stunning gem colors in our fall gardens. Raindrops sparkle in the bushes and the late spider webs. It's like a firework with which Nature waves us good-bye for its winter rest.

I have learned to use a lawn mower, and one of these days might bring the last mowing of the year. I have pruned our vines and cut our roses – except the last one that still springs another bud as if in rebellion against fall. My husband and I have raked hundreds of pounds of leaves and brought them to a composting place; the other half of the foliage is still up in the trees. And as I reflect this, I realize that having a garden has connected me even more with Nature than I used to be. I don't mind the mowing, the bending, the weeding, the pruning, the raking, the heaving. I harvest all these colors with my eyes and so many treats with my hands. Did I really only have a few wilting hanging boxes on a sixth-floor balcony in my former life? And did I just see another pound of golden and brown leaves sailing down onto our painfully raked lawn?

Clamming

I have always been one for seafood. Even as a little child in Germany, I loved clams – though nobody else in my family did. But my parents were wonderful about letting me try everything (that is, as long as it was not decidedly dangerous). My first clams were marinated, overcooked, and came out of a jar. Today, I'd probably disdain them, knowing what "the real deal" tastes like. But back then, clams were something exotic, only to be gotten in jars or cans from overpriced delis. Now, you can get them freshly frozen in German supermarkets. But to this day, clamming is a matter for the fishing industry in my mother country, certainly not for private people.

It was my husband, who introduced me to the possibility of clamming over here in Washington. First thing, we read up on the state's most unique mollusk, the geoduck (pronounce: goo-ee-duk), a delicacy that allegedly reaches retail prices up to 30 dollars a pound, depending where you buy it. Long story short – I think digging for it is more exciting than eating it. To find something looking like the tip of an elephant's trunk lurking out of the beach just above the waterline, then to shovel like crazy for the elusive giant that can become as old as 150 years, finally lying flat in the mud, arm stretched to the pit into the hole you have dug ... you get the picture. It's tough and dirty work for something that even as sashimi, to me, tastes tough and none too flavorful. I prefer the much smaller, but flavor-intense horse clams any time. They are a bit easier to dig (think elephant trunk tips covered with barnacles), a bit harder to clean (you need to skin them), and wonderful in stews, over pasta, and in chowders.

It took me a while longer to hear of razor clams. Maybe because I don't know too many clam diggers anyhow. Maybe because the grapevine from the Pacific Coast to Lakewood is a bit longer than the one from the Sound. We started watching tutorial movies and read up on those longish clams that are maybe the only ones you shoot. Just kidding, of course. But indeed, the alternative to digging for them with your hands or a shovel is a pipe with a handle and a hole somewhere on the top. And that tool is called a clam gun. Our first go at razor clams somewhere down in Long Beach was by hand and shovel – we failed. But we were able to purchase one of those guns, and at the last of light of that December night (we weren't seasoned as we are now and didn't have a source of light on us), we managed to dig our first three razor clams. We carried them to our abode in triumph, and I made fritters of them. I'll never forget the sweet, absolutely characteristic razor clam taste that night. Nor how our room still smelled of the cooking hours later.

These days, my husband and I check in November already that our clamming licenses are valid. We start inspecting the website of the Washington Department of Fish and Wildlife, hoping that razor clam season will open soon. Some years it has been at Christmas, some at New Year's Eve. We check tidal heights and times. We have found our favorite beaches, even favorite places to stay over the years. We don't look for fancy as long as there is a decent clam cleaning station. If there is a pantry kitchen to boot or a tavern in walking distance to warm us with a hot meal after clamming – all the better.

Strangely enough, the more demanding clamming conditions are, the more outstanding the memories. A couple of years ago, on a Christmas Day, we were staying at a tiny motel somewhere at the fringe of the Pacific dunes. It was a murky late afternoon, and as soon as we reached the beach with our gear, rain started battering down. Soon enough, we were wet through, as it came pelting down almost horizontally. A wave caught me by surprise on top of that and filled my rubber boots with a load of seawater. We kept digging. We wanted our limits. Once you are wet, you can't get wetter, right?!

What do I remember of that night? The beauty of countless people digging in the dark, carrying lanterns and wearing headlights – like fireflies on an icy, wet December night. The friendly chat with other clam diggers at the sheltered cleaning station, swapping cleaning tricks and recipes. How invitingly the lonely tavern was beckoning from down the road. How we found the last two seats at the bar and enjoyed the warmth and dry while warming up on a glass of red and waiting for our hot food.

To me, actual clamming is only part of an amazing and holistic adventure. I would never have experienced it in my German life. And I relish its entirety from the first plan in November to the last clam in the freezer.

Dancing Days

Dancing is big in Europe, and ball room dancing is something every kid attending a German grammar school usually learns at age 14 or 15 by attending a local dance school. I did, too, and enjoyed it that hugely that I taught my younger brother how to waltz, do the foxtrot, the blues, the cha-cha, and the rumba. Later I even joined a group which, besides singing traditional songs and having each member play an instrument, performed traditional German folk dances, but also historical ones such as minuets and quadrilles. American square dances were on the agenda as well. When my life took a busier route, I gave up on that group. But I still made time enough to go to a ballroom dance school twice a week in my home town. Apparently, I wasn't that bad either, as I constantly had to demonstrate the ladies' footwork, and I was even asked to be a guest dancer for some other classes. In other words, though I was never as good as the pros, I was passionate about moving to the sound of music with more than just "shaking it".

Being able to dance would come in quite handy even businesswise. The very first company I worked for always had ballroom dance music at their annual Christmas parties. And later business partners threw parties with a mix of ballroom dance and disco music. The trouble with it, as with most of such occasions anywhere: The men were none too keen to dance.

So, when I found that my American husband-to-be, who'd never had any dancing lessons, showed no aversion against moving his legs, I was thrilled. The very first time we listened to danceable music at his home, he simply offered me his hand, drew me towards him wordlessly, and off we stepped as if we'd been rehearsing for ages. Nothing complex, but simply in sync.

When we finally had our joint household here in Washington State, I found that my husband hadn't used dancing as a courting hook, but really enjoyed it. So, I suggested signing us up for ballroom dance lessons. I thought it would be easy. It was not.

The only school that taught ballroom dancing in the whole of nearby Tacoma was quite out of the way; during rush hour it would have taken us up to an hour to be there on time for classes. I checked with our local Community Center: Their classes had just been cancelled – only three other people had signed up. Finally, luck turned our way. Pierce College – sort of just around the corner from home – was offering ballroom dancing, and I signed us up. It would take only six evenings, and I was quite excited.

The first class started one early October night with only ten dancers, all of them in their fifties, except us who were younger by ten years then. Where were all the young people? Where were the military who have their big annual balls? Where were the high school students who were preparing for their senior proms? So many movie romances end with a ballroom scene –where were all the people who were supposed to dance at weddings, anniversaries, and Valentine's Days in real life?!

131

The dancing teachers were … ancient. But they were also exceedingly elegant, incredibly sprightly, and relentless in their teaching regime. What I had learnt in one and a half years at a German ballroom dance school, was squeezed into six nights here. The teaching method was different. I found I grew clumsier by the minute, trying hard not to step onto my husband's toes. I felt out of sync. I was supposed to touch no more than his shoulder and his hand during standard dances, whereas in Europe dancers' bodies touch each other in a way you could clamp a sheet of paper between them. Unless you're dancing a Latin American dance, of course. Dance step sequences were hailing down on us each hour and a half. It was tough to concentrate and to get everything right so quickly. Others in our class felt the same. Dancing was not really the fun it should have been.

Maybe that's why so few young people attend ballroom dance lessons here. Maybe that's why freestyle dancing is still growing in popularity, whereas dance schools in Europe, especially in Germany, are doing really well.

My husband and I still dance every once in a while. We just do our little routine, bodies touching, no ballroom steps. But it is fun – and very much in sync.

Radio Shows

I can go without television for a long time. My parents got their first set when I was turning 9. German television back then had only three channels, two national public ones and a regional public one. Until then, we had been listening to vinyl records and … to the radio.

We had some wonderful radio shows back in the day. I specifically remember a call-in one where people asked for or offered free used items, but also services. My mother answered one of those phone calls one day to help a family with two special needs kids. They developed a life-long friendship. The mornings of Christmas Eve were all about a two-hour Christmas tale featuring a fictitious dog called Knuddel (pronounce Khnooddle), and kids were asked to draw or paint pictures and send them in to win prizes. There were entertainment shows full of skits and trivia quizzes, and you could also call in and win a prize. There were Sunday lunchtime radio dramas in our local dialect – hilarious! And I especially loved the Saturday early night radio program on SDR1, presenting towns of our region with all their historical sights, orchestras, bands, and choirs, followed by the recoding of their church bells and a 10-minute bedtime drama for children. Not that we were in bed while listening. Often, we were on our way back from an all-Saturday outing, listening in the car.

With TV taking over and our listening, respectively watching habits changing, the radio programs changed, too. All my favorite radio shows vanished over the years. I stopped listening to the radio, only selectively watched TV, and mostly stuck my nose into books.

What a delightful surprise when I arrived over here in Washington State to find a lot of radio shows that strongly reminded me of my favorites from the 70s! The first time I was really aware of them was one Christmas Day out near Mowich Lake. It was snowing, and the roads were treacherous, to say the least. Basically, it was The Vinyl Café broadcasting a "Dave and Morley" Christmas story that saved my wits. Without it I might have been worrying my head off, wondering what would happen if we found ourselves stranded in the wilderness. Instead, I was laughing out loudly at the incredible twists of the tale, and I adored its Dickensian quality. Unfortunately, the last of this wonderful radio show of great stories was last aired in December 2017. I miss it greatly. If you have never listened into it, here's another chance: www.cbc.ca/listen/shows/vinyl-cafe.

I do not remember how many times my husband and I have been driving home to the story-telling of The Moth Radio Hour, real-life first-person stories that make you laugh, shudder, or simply remain pensive. Or listening in on the amazing scientific presentations of the Radio Lab. We make guesses and laugh along with the candidates of the news quiz show "Wait Wait ... Don't Tell Me" or the equally challenging "Ask me another" with comedian Orphira Eisenberg. And until recently, we regularly also tuned into Car Talk, where serious vehicle trouble usually got solved via remote diagnosis and turned into an incessant attack on the laugh muscles.

To be living near the Canadian border has definitely its assets concerning the availability of US *and* Canadian radio broadcasts. The musical side of the programs always provides listeners with interesting angles as well. You get the picture: When my husband and I are in the car, our radio is almost constantly on. And while he sees to the driving, my mind is allowed to drift to the incredible finesse of DNA or the secret of success, to struggle with answers to complex trivia questions, or to visualize the insanely funny stories about a couple called Dave and Morley. Ah, the old days back when! And the perfection they seemed to hold by just letting your mind picture things.

Working Out

I'm not a couch potato exactly. But when I hear the word "work-out", I shrink and try to bow out backwards. Maybe because the term "work" in work-out sounds like … well, something that is not entirely fun. Yet, I'm sure I'm not at the bottom of the scale of sporty people either. Work-outs simply don't have that much of an appeal to me.

As a child I was enrolled in a sports club with multiple programs. I was on a track and field team in first grade. I joined a gymnastics team in third grade but was uncomfortable, as the coach was male and I very shy. I hugely enjoyed my time as an aero wheeler in fourth grade – for whatever reason I excelled in that and received special training. I dropped sports clubs as school got more demanding. And I always hated school sports (twice a week, sometimes including swimming at a pool half an hour's walk away from school) – teachers were not really encouraging the ones who did not make the top ten everywhere.

I started power walking in my mid-thirties when I realized that I needed to keep in shape after having seen a particularly pudgy picture of mine in my own trade magazine. That was a turning point. For years, day after day, I went for an hourly walk through fields and forests, around lakes and along little rivers, anything that my suburban neighborhood in Germany offered, starting right at my front door. I found it exhilarating. My weight dropped, my mood rose, the landscape was changing on a daily basis. Moving became an addiction.

When I moved over here, to Steilacoom to be precise, I was happy to find walking routes galore around that pretty little Town on the Sound. Sidewalks made it a safe feat in most places, and the stunning vistas of the Sound and the Olympic Mountains were encouragement enough to go for my daily walks again. It takes no kick to the shin if you can walk a picturesque distance, starting and ending at your front door.

I have only come to really appreciate what I had until then after moving to where we are living now. Sure enough, our street has a sidewalk, but at the next big crossings that ends. When the weather is bad, the shoulders turn into muck, and the cars passing by spray you in addition. When the weather is good, the shoulders work for me, but I'm wary of the speed some drivers keep when passing me. In short, power walking from my front door has been a no-go from the start.

These days, I have to kick myself real hard to go for a walk. Because I have to take a ride to one of our parks first before I can start my walking routine at all. It takes a lot of spontaneity out of my work-out in nature. My husband has signed us up in a local gym. I'm not an indoor person, and the torturing machines and trainers inside remind me of my ambitious sports teachers and gyms of yore. I go along, but I have a hard time enjoying myself. I go there for the purpose, but not for the fun of it.

Thank goodness spring is coming along with mighty strides now, and I'm looking forward to long and explorative hiking tours with my husband. It's not going to be a daily thing, of course. But it will be a nice change in a routine of sit-ups on a mat, running on an elliptical trainer, and benching weights. Of late I have been seeing more and more signs pop up in Lakewood, announcing construction work. I keep hoping for more sidewalks, not just for the schoolkids, but for all citizens (And thank you, City of Lakewood, for doing so much of late!). Not just because it is so much safer and more sophisticated for a city than rough shoulders. But a power walk starting and ending at one's front door is really something that would give me a kick.

Beaches

The very first vacation I remember was when I was barely four. My family took a long train trip from Stuttgart to the Baltic Sea. I will never forget the sensual experience of that first seaside vacation, and maybe it has triggered my love for all things maritime. You can imagine how much it means to me to be close to the sea here in Western Washington. Even though the German seaside is so very different from the one we have here.

The first time I set foot on the beach in Ocean Shores, I was flustered that you actually had to look out for cars. I knew that there are beaches in this world where people drive instead of walking. The Netherlands have them as well. To me the concept, besides serving indeed as an alternative road from A to B, as it used to be before actual roads were built, is not enticing at all. I love beaches that are for pedestrians only. The tranquility and the purity of the air are like balm for body and soul. And a bit of exercise to reach the waterline from the beach entrance is quite welcome to me.

I have enjoyed countless vacations by the North Sea in my early twenties through my late 30s because the natural aerosol that you breathe during a long beach walk healed my hay fever and asthma for two years in a row. Better than any medication in fact. So, long beach walks were part of those vacations. And when I didn't walk, I hired a beach basket, that is a recliner inside a wicker shell or open tent. Some people used to build a sand wall all around theirs, decorated with stones and shells, as in "my home is my sandcastle". In later years this got more and more discouraged, as it adds to the erosion of beaches. And it can turn access to other beach baskets into quite a hike. Needless to say, the fun of beach baskets is unknown over here.

Instead I find people camp out on the Washington beaches with camping chairs and tables they carry along. Often enough an open fire is lit, and people sit around barbequing or cooking off clams and crabs. It looks extremely romantic at a day's end: these dots of fire at the bottom of the dunes, with people huddling around, the sound of laughter in the air. This is something I have never spotted anywhere in Germany.

Instead, you find sheds with glass-sheltered beer gardens right on the boardwalk in Germany. A hearty pea or barley stew, waffles, red berry compote with vanilla sauce, semolina pudding, sausages or deep-fried fish and chips are the most common fare. Farther towards town, you find cafés and restaurants on the esplanades. And often enough a concert shell with at least one concert a day during the tourist season.

Actually, I found one place in Western Washington where the flair with its dunes, boardwalks, and a town (in spite of the different style of architecture) filled with restaurants and tourist attractions comes pretty close to the German North Sea coast – Long Beach, the farther up north you go, the closer. It even smells similar! And the beach up north, at Leadbetter Point State Park, is entirely car-free, which makes it even more similar.

Oh, to enjoy a long beach walk and then go to a beach bar for fish and chips or salad, to imbibe the fresh, salty air and indulge in some simple seafood! When I was still a single in my late 30s back in Germany, I dreamed of retiring some place near the North Sea one day. Life has twisted things even a little more in my favor. Isn't it simply awesome that my home is only ten minutes from the Sound and maybe a 90 minutes' drive from the Pacific beaches now?! The language and the continent may be a bit different, and a lot of the coastline is way more dramatic than the one in Germany. But I wouldn't know which beaches I like better – either have their unique beauty.

Vacations

Germany is the world champion in traveling and has been so for ages. No matter how legendary Japanese traveling groups are around the world, snatching photos of everything, Germans have been there and done that before. Whether individually or in organized groups, whether high-fangled luxury trips to exotic places or eco-friendly social excursions, there's something for every German. Passports are a given, even though you have to pay for them. Compared to this: I recently heard somewhere that only ten percent of all US citizens own a passport at all and that only about 20 percent of the Washingtonians go on a summer vacation trip.

I've been a big-time traveler in my almost 42 German years, too. Exploring chunks of my mother country was as important to me as to get to know other European countries. I even peeked behind the Iron Curtain twice, in former Czechoslovakia. Business trips took me as far as the US West Coast and China. Once, I was even a wedding guest in Mumbai, India. Two bi-weekly vacations a year had become a standard to me as an adult single; and that left me another two weeks to spare for any kinds of family visits. That routine changed when my husband and I were courting. I flew out to England bi-monthly then, the actual trip taking a little above 3 hours and the tickets being a steal.

Coming here, I soon found that most people who travel are retirees. People who are still working seem to save up time and money to see their scattered family. Distances are simply incomparable to those within Europe, so those trips are often enough not just over a weekend. You *have* to turn your two weeks' vacations into family visiting time. You *have* to turn your holiday budget into the fare for flight tickets for the whole family – pretty expensive if you happen to have all of your relatives on the other side of the continent. No wonder that what remains of time and budget is turned into rather local vacationing.

In Western Washington, I think this is not even a challenge. It's pretty paradisiac with a stunning landscape, amazing wild life, and plenty of cultural opportunity. Who says you aren't experiencing a great vacation, while enjoying a picnic on a small rocky island beach on the first warm day of the year? Or when you play tourist and go browsing the stores of a pretty harbor town? Or hiking some mysteriously beckoning trails, or visiting some intriguing museums?

Maybe camping is not my first and foremost choice for overnight trips, though. I'm used to and prefer real beds, a nice private shower, and the comfort of my own kitchen instead of improvising cooking and doing the dishes over a camp fire. I love Nature, but I also love the accomplishments that mankind has produced to procure for creature comforts.

My first weekend vacation at a pretty little bed & breakfast place in the north of the Olympic Peninsula was an eye opener, though, as to why such vacations are often way out of league for the average American. The nice little suite with a fancy, but scant breakfast at the table d'hôte cost us the same amount as a room in a four-star hotel in Germany, huge fancy breakfast buffet included, or even an entire all-inclusive weekend holiday organized by a German travel agency. It made me wonder about the price/performance ratio in either country – and how many people here can afford such luxury.

Which might be another reason why staying in the area on your own terms can be quite the nicer, more comfortable summer vacation option. Share a steak with some friends at a sundown BBQ, catch fresh crab from the harbor dock with the neighbor down the road, or have a glass of red with a friendly, down-to-earth stranger over a camp fire. I could imagine worse.

Casinos

Germany is famous for its stylish casinos in Baden-Baden, Wiesbaden, and a few other cities. They used to be part of the Grand Tour rich Americans afforded their children to get a wider knowledge of the Old World in the 1800s and early 1900s. For Europeans who want to experience the non-plus-ultra in gambling, Las Vegas is *the* destination to travel to. Exploring Western Washington, I have come across a lot of casinos, too ... And I guess a history of attempted reconciliation might be what lies behind the density of these gambling houses here.

I remember my first casino experience with a German friend of mine back in my hometown of Stuttgart. The casino there had been open for just about ten years with Black Jack, Poker, Baccara, and Roulette tables. In Germany we call this the "Grand Game" – you can find the "Small Game" aka machine games in any gambling hole, often enough in the less reputable parts of towns, not necessarily as part of a regular casino. Nobody cares what you look like when you enter a place stuffed with slot machines. But you will be turned down at any "Grand Game" casino if your wardrobe doesn't match the dress code. It is jackets and ties for the gentlemen, dressy attire for the ladies. Ties can usually be borrowed at the entrance. A "Grand Game" casino afternoon or night in Germany (casinos open only for a limited time a day) is time to show yourself off, while gambling away at a table.

By the way, you must have an ID or a passport on you when you enter a German casino. It is not just about your age. They check at the entrance whether there is a search warrant for you and whether you are barred from another casino.

Entering a Washington casino, you have the Grand Game and the Small side by side. Sodas and coffee are free (I remember I paid for them in Germany), and apart from a doorman who probably checks your age or your harmlessness by sight there are no limitations. Meaning that you see people in fancy attire sitting at a machine next to people who obviously couldn't care less about clothing styles, as long as they are covered and warm. There is no showing off, no purpose of making this a special event in your life. It's rather a popping in and staying as long as the money holds.

I have seen large piles of chips lie on Roulette and Black Jack tables in Germany. In some cases, I felt as if I were observing a scene from a mafia movie. Faces were unreadable, attires immaculate, money was changed at the table – something that is usually only done when you hand over a higher amount of bills. Here, it seems to be a more casual affair, and the joy of winning is audible at the tables. A no-go over there in the Old World where you try to keep your poker face.

What else did I learn about the casinos here? That Asian casinos have only table games and that those have minimum stakes that can be pretty steep. That the casinos run by native Americans are only to be found on reservations, but that they include all the slot machines as well. That casinos on

146

reservations usually also have hotels, restaurants, and concert halls on site. And that, usually, you will find some famous names on the bill boards of such casinos. That one-cent-games are never one-cent-games, but that you have to check for the smallest bet to get the picture of how long a twenty-dollar-bill might last you. That there are people who stroke the monitors in order to achieve a better chance to win. That some people play up to three machines at the same time (I find this kind of passion for gambling a bit concerning). That a non-smoking area is not necessarily physically separated from the usually larger smoking areas. And that most cashiers are usually fun to talk to, especially when they are sitting alone in their cages and are not frequented by customers.

Do I gamble? Occasionally (which is rarely enough) I feel tickled by especially nicely designed machines, and I might lose a ten or a twenty. Usually I come out with as much as I went in with. No casino will ever become rich by me. I rather watch people, check the design or the theme of a complex, wonder about the employees and their stories ...

And yet I feel some satisfaction when I see that a reservation is taking pride in opening a new community center or a supermarket, a lodge or some other improvements that look nice and maybe bring them further income. It's little enough of a quid pro quo. So, when I lose a game, I keep thinking it might be for somebody else's good after all. Maybe that is naïve. Be it so.

147

Music

I come from a music addicted family and married into another music addicted one. For both branches that means a history of concerts, wherever we were able to grab one. And yet, our respective experiences could probably not be more different.

I grew up on almost only smooth jazz and classical music. I saw my first opera in Stuttgart, Germany, at the opera house when I was eight. We were all dressed to the tees and after the doors closed, everybody just sat and listened in awe. It was an easy opera to watch, Engelbert Humperdinck's "Hansel and Gretel", and the stage set was marvelously traditional. After that event, I started saving up pocket money for buying classical records.

Looking back, my circle of friends was entirely stage-struck in the traditional department as well. I was probably the only one who didn't have regular private music lessons due to any lack of ambition until I was 15. Some of my friends were avid piano players or even ballerinas. In my mid-teens, my music teacher told me my voice ought to be trained professionally and hooked me up with a concert singer. My perspective changed big time from being the rapt girl in the audience to being a soloist on stage or up in organ lofts. I learned how many rehearsals go into one tiny piece of less than five minutes until all the orchestra instruments co-relate with each other and the singer. Until the acoustics have been figured out and the tempi and volumes are adapted to the location. I ditched my social life as an evolving teenager to be on stage, to maybe become a professional singer one day, to breathe music four to five hours a day at home, not counting music lessons at school or with private singing and piano teachers.

Well, I didn't become a professional opera singer, as we all know by now, but I was able to make use of my knowledge in my first year as a journalist. I wrote for a local paper's culture section. Thanks to my dancing friends, I knew enough about ballet to appreciate pirouettes and lifting figures, jetés and pliers danced to the music of any era. Talking to opera stars, prima ballerinas, jazz musicians, and actors after shows became my every weekend enjoyment. It didn't matter to me whether they were big stars or fervent up-and-coming artists. They gave their all. That was all that counted. That is why I am still stage-struck whenever I sense somebody giving their heart and soul to their performance.

I met who would become my husband over the guitar-music and voice of an Irish singer-songwriter in my hometown. We were both enjoying the tunes hugely, and our first encounter was actually a remark about the amazing quality of that artist. The rest of the conversation was about music, books, movies, and our life philosophy – but music definitely started it.

I visited my first rock concert the summer I arrived in Washington State. Rock music had never been on my concert list anywhere before. I was a bit tense at first. It was a little like going to the opera for the first time. I had no clue what kind of a crowd I would be surrounded by. My husband had introduced

149

me to the music we'd be listening to via records and playing the guitar, explaining texts and watching interviews with the band. And then, one balmy summer night, we actually were out there at the White River Amphitheater in Enumclaw. It was a happy crowd we plunged into, one generation next to the next, people singing along, playing air instruments. The stage show was colorful and enjoyable. I found myself humming along with one or two songs to my own surprise.

Since then, we have been to jazz concerts and musicals all over the place. We have seen and heard rock stars that I grew up with only on the radio. And I have admired amateur stage productions around here that had the same ambition as the big names – to satisfy their audience. And they did.

We love to listen to classical music on the radio every once in a while. I still sing a lot, opera or oratorio arias and lieder, sometimes still at a church or social event, but mostly to myself and when I'm doing the dishes at home. Still, the best moments to me are when my husband grabs his guitar and rocks it. That always reminds me of our first encounter and of how music – no matter what kind – can bring different worlds together.

Farmers Markets

I have been waiting and anticipating them for months – the farmers markets in the South Sound region with all their individual perks. I have, by no means, been to all of them. I love the one in Olympia for its versatility. But Olympia is annoying to get to through the I-5 corridor, and we have pretty interesting farmers markets a bit further up north as well. Similar, yet quite different from the German farmers markets I grew up with and enjoyed for the majority of my life.

Actually, in Germany we don't even call them "Bauernmarkt" (pronounce 'bowern-markt, i.e. farmers market) in the Stuttgart region. As they are supplied by farmers almost exclusively, calling them that would be kind of redundant, I guess. It's "Wochenmarkt" (pronounce 'vaugh-hen-markt) as in a weekly market – and in quite a few cases they are happening even twice a week. If you ever have the opportunity to visit the Stuttgarter Markthalle, yes, a market hall, you will see a splendid example of early 20th century German Art Deco architecture featuring the most elegant specialty stands for native and foreign foods, surrounded by a gallery of exclusive designer stores and a renowned farm-to-table restaurant. That market hall is open almost on a daily basis.

But it doesn't have to be that upscale. The bi-weekly market in my little suburb featured a fishmonger in a food-truck-like vehicle. In similar trucks, you would find bakers and butchers. A Greek stand was my pièce de résistance with at least a dozen kinds of differently marinated and stuffed or unpitted olives, stuffed vine leaves and pepperoncini, octopus as well as shrimp salads, and marinated beans of all sorts. Flowers and native fruit and vegetable stands with their striped or unicolor canopies completed the colorful picture around town hall beneath the steeple of a neogothic church.

My first year over here, I wasn't able to find a single farmers market. I didn't try very hard either, as everything was so new to me anyhow and I was exploring sort of all over the place. But over the months I found myself able to focus more on such things and, behold!, the Steilacoom Farmers Market with its evening concerts became a favorite venue. All-white canopies lend this summer event quite a festive appearance. The Lakewood Farmers Market, fairly newer but outlasting the Steilacoom one by some weeks every year, has concerts right on site, next to City Hall. There are even farmers from as far as Yakima apparently, bringing in colorful fruit and veggies that might not yet have been harvested west of the Cascades.

My very favorite farmers market though is the one up in Proctor. I don't know – maybe it's because it reminds me the most of a European Wochenmarkt, being in the middle of the lively business district with its quaint mom and pop stores and restaurants. It is colorful. No stand resembles the next. The variety of offers is quite unusual. You find fiddleheads and baskets of mushrooms of the more uncommon varieties in early spring, duck and rabbit (nose to tail), artisan breads, fish, flowers, pickles, plants, mixers that work for cocktails as well

152

as for cooking ... It is not huge, but it feels as if it embraces and centers on more unusual, uncommon produce. It speaks to my senses somehow more than other markets. So far, I have never managed to go up one side and then come down the other (yes, it is just one street section!) without a bag of loot for my kitchen. And I have been creating rabbit dishes, fried cabbage in duck fat, sizzled fiddleheads, and mixed a bell pepper potion into a gin and Seltzer as well as into a vegetable stew. Every once in a while, I entreat my husband to spend an hour up there of a Saturday morning to explore and indulge.

It's so nice to see farmers markets spring up everywhere here in the country. It feels good to drive by a farm and know that you just had some of their produce on your plate just the other day. It connects you to the soil and the people who work it. It makes you more aware of what you are eating. It supports an industry that is working with Nature and often enough has to battle it, too. Maybe it's why a visit to farmers markets has such a special vibe for me. It's the end of a production journey for the farmer and the beginning of my food exploration. Maybe it's that why we are smiling at each other, as any purchase is rewarding for either of us.

Dining Out

Have you ever wondered why Americans abroad are pretty quickly recognized as such as soon as they enter a restaurant? Especially in Germany? Even though they might not have a military haircut and not speak overly loudly? Here are some fun facts that I discovered over the years.

When I go out with my husband, he usually opens the restaurant door for me and lets me enter first. I had to wrap my European head around this when we courted. Because German men (and if the host is a woman, that woman) would certainly enter first – in order to check the grounds by sight. Maybe it's too full, maybe somebody is behaving raucously, maybe whatever … It's to make sure that the lady/guest doesn't run into any uncomfortable situation.

In a German restaurant, in most cases you choose a table and sit down; in high-end restaurants, somebody might approach you and ask whether you have booked a table or whether they might find you one. You usually don't find anybody in a waiting area or a bar lounge as over here or somebody calling out your name when it's your turn to be seated. Your *first* name at that! Germans go by their last names in everyday life unless you are their friend and have offered you to call them by their given name. Unimaginable that a service person should call you by your Christian name. You won't ever get to know theirs either, by the way.

As soon as I'm sitting down in a restaurant over here, I usually get asked what I'd like to drink. It keeps irritating me.

I mean, I only just sat down. I don't have a clue what beverages they have, and they are usually serving me a glass of ice water I never asked for (or am ever going to drink) anyhow. So, give me a minute! Don't expect that free service in Germany, by the way. You will be handed a beverage menu, and they might leave you to ponder it until you signal them. Oh yes, you can! Sometimes you even have to. A slightly raised arm and a nod will call your waiter or waitress to the table. Over here, I have been hovered over by waiters sometimes to the point when I felt I couldn't even have a private conversation without being interrupted by the question whether everything was alright.

Another fact? We probably all know by now that Germans, when eating with a knife and fork, will never switch hands and that Americans betray their nationality the instant they have cut their food by laying down their knife and switching their fork to that hand. Maybe it's only half a joke that there is a reason for the latter – to have one hand ready at the gun under the table.

Reordering drinks with your finger count? You will have to be careful whether your finger count works with the nation you're in. Showing a thumb and a finger in German means "two", the first three fingers mean "three", thumb in and four up … well, you get the picture. Allegedly, during WW II more than one American spy has been caught because of tiny differences like these.

You are finally in the last stages of your meal? Here in the US, you are being asked whether you would like anything else, often while you are still chewing. If you say "No", your waiter will slip you (or the person they assume will pay) the check. It's the signal that your table is up and waiting for the next person. Unthinkable in Germany. There, you might even sit and wait until they are sure you are done. And they will not deliver you the check until you have decided you are finished and want to pay. Theoretically, you can sit over another glass of your beverage for the rest of the evening, and nobody will question it.

Doggy bags have become a possibility only in few German restaurants these days. Servings are usually manageable. Here, in most restaurants I find doggy bags an annoying necessity unless you want to waste the food. Basically, I am not keen on leaving a nice restaurant, all dressed up and holding a plastic bag of food. I dislike reheating restaurant left-overs – they never taste as nice as they were when first served. And when I'm going out, I want to experience a one-time special – not the regurgitation of a memory by ways of half-eaten Styrofoam box contents the next day. Therefore, I find myself sharing one dish with my husband at most times. Which limits choices for either of us just because the portions are oversized.

Of course, there are always exceptions to the rules. But they are hard to find. And as an American in Germany you will find yourself struck by some weird experiences while eating out just as much as I was when I first traveled here. I have gotten used to restaurant culture both sides of the Atlantic. But you are guessing right when you assume that I find that the one overseas is more pleasant – even though, as you sit down, you get a glass of tap water for free over here.

Reading

Have you ever thought over how much your reading shapes your mindset, but how it is also defined by what nation you belong to? Obviously, most people's first books will be in their mother tongue. Mine weren't. And my favorite was an American one, "One Morning in Maine".

I became a lover of English literature as soon as I learned English in fifth grade. I began to favor Shakespeare over Goethe, loved Austen as much as Fontane, and preferred modern English and Irish literature by far over their German contemporaries. Our local library – I held a 2-Marks-an-hour-job there for a year when I was 14 – had only so many books in English. When Amazon started business over in Germany, I had boxes of English, Irish, and American literature delivered in an insane monthly to bi-weekly rate – and I devoured each and every book, some of them twice.

Then came my emigration. I had a library of about 2,000 books. I wouldn't be able to dump all these on our new home, and my moving container was limited in size also. It hurt. Over the first yard of cookbooks I gave away I actually bawled. It was easier to hand over a car load of 500 English books to the near US barracks' library, so other people would enjoy them.

When I came here, I found to my surprise that with your rent you automatically acquire the right to a library card. (In Germany you have to buy that extra.) I'll never forget the day when I, having read pretty much every last book my husband owns, ventured into the Steilacoom Library. Its size was speaking to me; so was its peaceful atmosphere and the gorgeous etched window at its back.

But where to start? What to read? I had a few recommendations from newspapers or magazines, of course. What did Americans read, so I was not entirely thrown if they wanted to discuss it with me? I'm not talking Thoreau, Hawthorne, Dickinson, Melville, Dreiser, and all these classics. That entire canon I had been working through and hugely enjoying while studying general and comparative literature at Stuttgart University. I wanted current literature. Who was considered important? Who en vogue?

That day I set up a rule for myself that I have stuck to for more than seven years now. I will try and read every single book that turns up on my way through the fiction author alphabet of A through Z. I will skip fantasy as I have had my feed of classic legends in the Old World. Accidentally, I once ended up with a book that I found had less than a quarter of its page count for a plot, the rest was comparable to "Fifty Shades of Grey". No, I'm not into that kind of novels either.

Over the years, the most amazing books found their way home with me – genres and topics I might never have picked if I hadn't imposed the book-by-book-rule on myself. I have discovered fantastic Sci-Fi-novels by authors that I have never heard of anywhere. I've read fun romance and deep semi-autobiographic novels. I have learned about history and geography, about different ethnicities and their life in the US or their mother countries. I have read books friends of mine have published. Ever so often I sneak in non-fiction, too. And sometimes, one of the friendly Steilacoom librarians discusses one or the other book with me in a half-whisper, so we don't disturb those who work at the computers.

These days, I've reached the letter "F", and only a week ago I pulled another gap into the library shelf, taking along five books in a row. If I keep reading at this speed, I'll be finished in 20 more years. By that time, the shelves before probably hold an entire quarter century of new books and new authors. Maybe I will be able to start with the letter A again. Maybe I will find different "rules" for myself. At any rate, it's reading-fun full of good surprises and experiences. And if you come across a bigger gap on a shelf out there ... maybe it was me who has just gotten herself some more food for thought.

Volunteering

Volunteering has always been something more rewarding to me than a nuisance. Though in Germany it had way less meaning to me and I was hardly able to do any, once I was a full-time journalist. But even at school camps, I found it more fun to help dry the dishes or cut onions for 60 kids and teachers than to play the umptieth game of table tennis without really connecting. Whereas you forge bonds while crying over ten pounds of hot onions with a couple of other volunteers, believe me. In my early twenties, I also served as a church elder for some years – I don't think the term "elder" was appropriate at the time though ...

When I came over here, volunteering meant integration to me. It meant becoming part of a bigger concept, paying forward, but also getting back friendship and neighborliness. Nobody except my husband and some of his friends had been knowing I was coming over, after all. So, nobody was exactly rolling out a red carpet, offering me a job on arrival or anything similar. Neither did I expect that.

But, one day I found this door hanger at our front door, recruiting new members for a local historical museum and asking whether I was interested in volunteering. I was not sure that I had the capability of doing what they were expecting. It *was* a historical museum, after all, and my knowledge of local history was only recently gained from a couple of books and websites. But, lo and behold, I was invited to become a docent and got trained. I was invited to join their Education Committee also. Later, I was asked to become the office manager (which position I filled for a while). And for six years, I have been a trustee with the museum as well.

Also, I filled in a civilian volunteer position on a military base as the liaison between military families and a local squadron command for a couple of years. I will never forget the day the commander asked me in and offered me the position, and she didn't care at all that I – at that time – was still a German citizen with only a US green card. It was an immense honor to me, and quite a few friendships I made back then are holding to this day, military *and* civilian.

In 2018, I wore another hat. I had been asked by the organizers of the 6th Annual Lakewood Film, Arts, and Book Festival to help create and coordinate the September event's first author/book section. It was fun being asked as one of the exhibiting authors and to be able to bring to the table what I imagined the other exhibiting authors might also need. It was a lot of work – but the best reward came when the doors opened and everything ran as smoothly as could be.

Looking back on my volunteering tasks in Germany and those here, there are some differences. My tasks over there were minor as a school kid. And later, with 14-hour-days, work-weekends and lots of traveling, I simply didn't have the time or energy to volunteer anymore. Over here, I had lots and lots of time on my hands. It's becoming less and less again, as I'm writing on a regular basis again, of course. But counting myself as semi-retired, I find that volunteering is a mighty good opportunity for any teenager or adult who can cut him- or herself loose for a couple of hours a week to achieve a greater goal that helps a community. Looking around, I hardly see anybody in my circle of friends who doesn't volunteer. Overseas, it would have been a different story.

Ah yes, and then there are the awards volunteers get recognized with over here. Not sure they are handed out as freely (or as heart-felt) over in Germany as they are here. In my very first year I received one as part of a group that had a major impact on a museum program. Later, still a German citizen, I received US military awards on the squadron level, but also on that of an entire Air Force Base.

I have to admit that all of these awards fill me with pride and with gratitude. But the one thing that even feels better is that volunteering has made me part of programs and concepts that helped others and changed things in communities. To wrap it up in a nutshell: Volunteering is as much for others as it is for yourself. And it's never become clearer to me anywhere else than in my new home.

Hiking

When I was a kid in Germany, my family went off hiking to the Black Forest or to the Swabian Alb, low mountain ranges close to my hometown, Stuttgart, on a regular basis. Either a newspaper clip or a hiking book was placed in my mother's shoulder bag, and usually they were day trips. I was not sure I liked hiking at all, as it took me away from my books and set me apart from our neighborhood children even more. They were all non-hikers with parents who couldn't have cared less about family activities such as that.

My parents always saw to it that the hikes held something special that we children would find enjoyable: waterfalls with bridges, little gorges, brooks to follow, old grist mills, caves, fortress ruins. If there was a village en route, we could be sure to be treated to an ice cream popsicle purchased usually in its only grocery store or Gasthof (pronounce 'gust-hoh-f, meaning guest court, i.e. tavern). Our shortest hikes amounted to around nine miles, our longest were around 16. We sported hiking shoes and wooden hiking sticks. My father carried a rucksack stuffed with homemade sandwiches, cut-up apples, a thermo with herb tea, breaded and fried cold schnitzels, and a jar of my mom's yummy potato salad. The load was topped off with a blanket for picnicking. Picnic places were chosen randomly around noon – it could be a bench by the trail, it could be in the middle of a meadow.

The absolute highlight of those hikes usually lay at the end of such a long walk. As soon as we had deposited our

164

walking sticks and the rucksack back in our car, our family would head for either coffee and cake at a local café or for supper in a village tavern. Going out was very special for us, as it occurred very rarely. It was the carrot my parents knowingly or unknowingly dangled in front of my unwillingness to hike.

Years later, when I was vacationing by myself, I found that hiking was a marvelous way to explore the surroundings of my vacation spots. I walked all around the North Sea islands I visited, I hiked in the Bavarian Forest. I hiked on Crete and Corfu in Greece. I hiked the entire coastal path of the island of Guernsey, England. I bought special hiking shoes. I bought myself fancy rucksacks. I bought hiking books and maps. A vacation without any hiking didn't feel much like a vacation in the end. I didn't even need any popsicles in between anymore. A tavern at the end of a hike was still very welcome though.

When I moved over here, I was more than pleasantly surprised about the marvelous hiking opportunities that are offered in Western Washington (and probably in quite a few other places in the States as well). I was even happier that my husband turned out to be an avid hiker who always found a way to picnic in a comfy and cozy manner – even when the ground was snowy! The trails in the mountains are lovingly kept. You find benches in places you'd not even expect. There are sign posts at every trail junction. Special vista points are pointed out. Charts are available at any crucial point to see where you are and which options you might want to choose next.

Whereas in Germany the only wildlife I spotted during hikes were maybe a red squirrel or a woodpecker – the country is way more densely populated and tamer – here in Washington, we spot chipmunks and gray squirrels, marmots and mountain goats, deer, and even bears. There are waterfalls and brooks to my heart's delight anywhere in this part of the country. I don't really miss the fortress ruins – we run into old mine entrances and ghost towns every once in a while.

I sometimes wish for an old little village that throws itself into our path though. Or a mountain cottage-cum-tavern in the middle of the wilderness. It is these contrasts I realize today that make the memory of a hike even more vibrant. As to picnics – my husband is a marvelous provider of rucksack surprise feasts. And finding a fun place to eat at after a long hike has never been an issue either. Though we find – cooking together at home after a hike is even more fun!

Writing

Sometimes I get asked what it takes to be a writer. The answer is: Write!

I also get asked when I decided to become a writer. I never did. It decided me. Before I could write, I told stories to my kid brother. As soon as I was able to spell, I borrowed my parents' mechanical typewriter and hacked out stories. I became a professional writer after finishing university. I wrote and published my first book at age 25. Today, I'm a columnist and a novelist ... something I had dreamed of becoming. Something I had never thought I could become. And I'm doing it all in a foreign language.

Germany has a rich tradition of writing. I was taught to read medieval German and fought myself through Hartmut von Aue, Walter von der Vogelweide, and Wolfram von Eschenbach. I have to admit I liked Chaucer's witty Canterbury Tales better. I prefer Shakespeare over Goethe and Schiller. And I like modern British and American literature way better than most of what my mother country has to offer. So, where is the difference in writing?

I don't think it is the language in which a text is written that determines the lightness of the tone. Though, obviously, the English language lends itself marvelously for double entendres with all its homophones and even homonyms, i.e. words that sound the same or are spelled the same, but have different meanings. Over decades of reading I rather seemed to detect a different mindset. German authors of renown are almost always dead-serious and often pessimistic. Few exceptions like Theodor Fontane come to my mind. And if they are funny or light-hearted, they are often not considered as worthwhile reading. It's almost like a binary class system of literature. I do not find the same in the English language.

Literature is something that is entertaining and educating. Once you apply this definition, I find a lot falling into this category, with manuals of my kitchen utensils, sheet music, and the telephone book outside the category. And I keep thinking of all these people writing away, day after day, for a living. To tell stories. To share facts or messages. To incite kindred spirits. I for myself have decided to carry a positive voice. This is why you won't find any huge controversial topics in my column "Home from Home". This is why my everyday-life Wycliff novels paint normal people struggling, but always reach a happy ending.

Writing is a tough bread. When I started out, I received 10 cents per line and about ten dollars per appointment. I worked like crazy. I could have found myself a job that would have paid better for less engagement. But it had to be writing. In the end I had a well-paying job – and I had a hard time making my texts in a trade magazine educating *and* entertaining. Today, ... well, I'm not one of the big authors, and I'm none of the famous ones either... So, you get the picture. I keep writing. I am happy about kind responses and one or the other praising Amazon review.

It's passion that churns me and all of my fellow writers. This weekend, you will be able to encounter over 40 authors at the Shirley McGavick Center of Clover Park Technical College (yes, I will be there, too). You will find that quite a few fit several genres, some with one and the same book, others by producing for different genres. Ask them what makes them write. And ask yourself – why are you reading?

In the end, a book is the magic world where the mind of one writer meets the minds of many readers. A book will survive the writer, but its potential to reach readers will be there as long as it exists. Maybe that is part of the fascination.

Maintenance

Let's face it – maintenance is not my strongest talent. That's probably because I come from a family that never owned a home (landlords took care of maintenance) and that was rather on the academic side of life. Also, there are quite a few regulations what you are permitted to maintain or repair where and when in Germany – which limits a lot of technical ambitions to simply knowing who delivers which service. I knew how to connect ceiling lamps and how to fix minor items at my sink. I knew how to repair or correct flaws in tiles and how to fill in drilling holes in a wall. As for anything more complex, I knew where to find maintenance and repair specialists via phone book and employ them for anything major.

Coming to the US, I realize how people take care of a lot of things themselves, even if they are only renting. Having a garden for the first time in my life has changed a lot for me. I have learned how to rake and discard 500 pounds of leaves every fall – oh my, it's almost that time of the year again, right?! My German landlords hired a landscaper for things like that. And I hugely enjoy mowing our lawn – it's meditative, and I see what I have worked on as in an instantaneous reward. My husband cleans our gutters – and every time he does so, I am half-dying with worry he might fall off the ladder as he wields a hose and broom, walking the ladder with his legs.

Only recently I read that the daughter of friends of ours is really into her own car repairs. I never knew more than how to change a tire (theoretically) and exchange a bulb or a spark plug. That's pretty much all people in Germany do unless they are real car geeks. Anything more complex is delivered to a body shop. I never had a clue to which degree anybody can take apart a car and repair it on their own grounds until I saw it done to my own. My husband is a wiz with mechanical and engineering problems, and he has taught me a lot by explaining things in a simplistic way. I still don't dare do any more maintenance than help cleaning our cars. But I think I have gained a lot more knowledge about technical problem analysis when I hear a sound that shouldn't be there. Or when a light goes off that should not be lit.

Neighbors of ours have built an entire beautiful shed from scratch in their backyard. Others added an awning over their porch. Some paint their house all by themselves. I am pruning my bushes in fall.

What is it that makes Germans go to specialists and pay them rather than tend to maintenance themselves as so many Americans do? Is it a sense of self-doubt in one's ability to accomplish a hands-on task? The ambition to have everything done perfectly? Or simply that maintenance involves getting yourself dirty sometimes? A distinction between blue-collar and white-collar society even? The absence of fun in a task that prolongs the life of something you own or even just rent? I know some American guys who open up their car hoods just to look whether they can find anything that might need repair even if they have just overhauled the entire vehicle.

Admittedly, I am still too German to see the enjoyable side of maintenance work, but American enough to get myself dirty and feel pride once a maintenance project is done. I often feel I might not be up to the job because I was never taught how to. With my husband around I'm slowly getting better at simply trying. Also, I realize that I still hesitate to get myself dirty – I was raised to be spic and span and speckless at all times. In my American life, I find myself immersing into all kinds of pastimes that leave me a load of dirty clothes by the washing machine. So, why not add maintenance?!

Well, fall house and yard maintenance is coming up. Time to roll up my sleeves and get prepared. Is there still enough gas in our lawn mower?

Crafting

In a little over a month, we will be celebrating Thanksgiving again, and then the final rush into Christmas preparations begins. Which means writing dozens of Christmas cards and sending them out in time before the cut-off date. Which means that *now* is the time to start crafting Christmas decorations and Christmas cards. The latter a thing I never did back in Germany.

Sometimes I think it strange that I was working as a journalist with the creative crafts industry for almost 16 years way back when, but never really found the time to create my own Christmas cards. I did make my own little floral advent arrangement every year. But no Christmas cards. I had all the materials on hand, free samples from manufacturers who wanted me to experience their products outside their workshops to which I also was generously invited. I acquired skills in a whole lot of different techniques. But I rarely put them to use. There was a simple reason: I was working 12- to 14-hour-days, writing, organizing events, often traveling at that. Coming home, I didn't feel leisurely enough to create even more. And let's face it – crafting dozens of cards tends to become work when under time pressure.

My life was turned upside down when I came over here. Suddenly I had all the time in the world, all the materials at hand, and amazing craft stores all around into the bargain. I started to paint again until the walls in our house were covered with what I call regular art and my attempts on canvas. I began to create decoupage objects again – little boxes, coasters, even a guitar pedal. I helped with the Kids Club at the Steilacoom Historical Museum and introduced some fun papercraft and painting projects there. At one time I even introduced a group of ladies to Heritage Crafts – we decorated wooden Kleenex boxes with tole painting.

These days, I am grabbing my boxes of crafting paper, blank greeting cards, stickers, stamps, glitter, embossing powders, special effect pens, silhouette scissors, punches, and ribbons again and set to work. Around 50 greeting cards are waiting to be made. I haven't decided on a specific look yet. Maybe, I'll cut some windows into the cards with a die-cut machine. Maybe I'll add some song lyrics. Maybe I will create something 3D that is not too difficult to squeeze into an envelope and that won't obstruct a post office's stamping machine.

Later, it will be time to think about advent decorations. The First of Advent will be only on December 2 this year. German private households usually don't start decorating before Eternity Sunday – so there's a relaxed timeline. Maybe, our Christmas tree will go up at the same time, for the sake of my husband's American traditions – decorated with a load of handcrafted ornaments made from wood, from beads and wire, or simply painted.

But wait – it's only October. Why run ahead that far?! It's just about the Christmas cards and some wax candles for now (because I know how quickly nice, non-perfumed stump candles sell out). We still have some beautiful weeks of fall lying ahead – with pumpkin decorations, colorful foliage, scarecrows, grapes, asters, maybe some crows in the medley … or a turkey. I better see to it that my decoration for Thanksgiving is set up nicely. A floral arrangement on the doorstep, some small bouquet on the dining table … Only the other day I found a pretty candle arrangement that I had crafted a few years ago and that by now has come unglued. I might want to craft something like that again. If I'm in the mood to do so. There is no hurry, no pressure there. Everything will fall into place – in the end, holidays are grounded in one's heart. If they were only all about decoration, what sense would they make?

Food

Piece of Cake

I'm not a baker. I am not even much of a cookie eater. In short, I have an under-developed sweet-tooth. Still, the other day, when a friend of mine called me to ask whether I would bake a batch of cookies for a semi-private event, I said yes.

Of course, I needed a hint as to what to bring. I didn't want to be the umptieth person delivering the umptieth three dozens of the same kind of baked goods. "Chocolate chip cookies, peanut butter cookies, or snickerdoodles," my friend said. "You can always use a ready mix, too." Now, I might not be a baker, but I have a home maker's honor to defend. From scratch it would have to be, of course!

As I hung up, I suddenly had second thoughts. Not about the baking itself. About the kinds of cookies requested. Why? They are so American, that this German immigrant has once or twice tasted, but never made them. Ever. Peanut butter is something I prefer in savory dishes. Chocolate chip cookies are definitely not my kind, unless there is more than "just" chocolate to them. And snickerdoodles, though certainly delectable, still make me wonder about their name. Don't they sound like something dangerously potent from Alice's Wonderland?! (Apparently though, the name derives from the German word "Schneckennudel", but that coiled yeast pastry has nothing in common with its American cousin.)

Anyhow, I found myself discarding two kinds of cookies from my mind, deciding to give the cinnamon ones a try. To be on the safe side, I'd also make a batch of my

179

peppermint chocolate chip cookies. Comes near enough the real deal, right? And just in case nobody would find my first try with American cookies good enough, I'd bring a batch of German cookies for compensation. At least, I know what they have to be like, since I grew up on such.

Vanillekipferl? Nusshoernchen? Kokosmakronen? Heidesand? Elisenlebkuchen? I had daymares about burnt cookies. Half-baked cookies. Cookies too crumbly. Cookies too sweet. Cookies too exotic. Finally – eureka! Alpenbrot it would be, that flavorful something slightly kindred to Magenbrot and gingerbread, inconspicuously brown, almost shapeless, but oh so flavorful. Lovingly glazed with a thin sugar coating while still hot. Stored away in a tin for a few days to gain more chewiness. I might not win any ribbon with my American cookies, but maybe my German ones would get me a smile or two.

Here now, I find myself baking three times three dozens of cookies instead of only one batch of one dozen, with temperature rising to the 90s outside – and quite near that inside the house. Though I am so not a baker. And … ah, you already know all of the above.

Integration can be a challenge to an immigrant from half a world away. And it may or may not be a piece of cake even in the case of a batch of 36 cookies.

Barbecue

When I grew up, the term Barbecue or BBQ for putting something onto the grill was yet unknown in Germany. My family, as so many Germans, used to live in apartment buildings from anything between 6 to over 20 units, and barbecuing was something strictly regulated there. Every unit had a fixed number of BBQ opportunities per annum. I think it was around six; it may have been ten. And it made somewhat sense in these close surroundings. Back in the early 70s, most German grills were charcoal ones. In a house with even just six units, that would make up to 60 nights of charcoal smoke and ashes flying into other apartments' windows and balconies.

For whatever reason, my parents were not into grilling anything at home at all. I never asked them why. I know they didn't like the smell. I imagine they didn't care much for cleaning messy charcoal ashes, either. They had had their share of lugging wood and coal from cellars to top floor apartments to keep our home warm and of carrying the cold ashes three staircases down again. They might have simply gotten to the point when they were done with the "fun" of building any kind of fire. But I remember us using the pits in picnic areas where we were awkwardly holding sausages stuck onto big sticks we had gathered in the forest and sharpened to a point over the open fire. I *loved* BBQs. Maybe all the more so because they were such a rarity.

Later, visiting with family in the US state of Maine, I encountered the typical American kettle grill for the first time.

Every once in a while, during my two all-summer stays, my Uncle Del would put the hugest steaks I'd ever seen (today I know they were London broil cuts) over a carefully built and patiently waited for charcoal glow. Thinly sliced, only salted and peppered, these meats, along with my Aunt Isa's incredibly delicious mushroom and herb rice, are still memorable. Just talking about them, makes my tongue taste them again. These BBQs would have to last me for long years after.

Everything changed when I met my husband. Back then, one night during my first visit at his temporary home in England, he surprised me with a BBQ meal. And it was not a simple piece of meat, either, just flung onto the grill. It was a kabob, lovingly assembled on a spit with onions and bell peppers, seasoned top-notch. We were watching bunnies in his garden, while laying the table on the patio. We observed the horses on the neighboring pasture, while cobs of corn, wrapped in aluminum foil, were steaming away under a glaze of butter, salt, and pepper. And when everything was done, a turn on a vent and a flick on a knob shut off the grill immediately. No dust, no ashes, just cleaning off the grill residue later. And the culinary result? I was hooked. One of our wedding gifts would be a BBQ grill, by the way – from the above-mentioned uncle and aunt.

We are still trying to perfect our grilling style these days, way beyond kabobs, steaks, and sausages. I have learnt to overcome my fear of fire and am quite capable of outdoor-steaming the crab we catch in Puget Sound during crabbing season. We plank fish. We grill shrimp and veggies. We are getting quite savvy about grilling times and produce thickness, respectively density. We rub and marinate. We coat and glaze. We discuss, and we time as we work side by side. We observe birds and squirrels in our back yard, while barbecuing. We sip a glass of wine, while watching the sundown.

Barbecuing is still very special to me. It might never become a normal everyday thing for me. I love the smells and flavors. I love the relaxed atmosphere. Recently, with temperatures up in the 80s and beyond, our BBQ got a temporary rest. But oh, does the German child in me look forward to when the vent gets turned, the knob clicked, and the switch flicked on again!

Sweet Memories

I grew up on exactly one candy a day as a little child. None if I hadn't behaved. It was not tough. It was what I was used to. Christmas, Easter, and birthdays therefore meant something extraordinary for their mere abundance of sugar treats. And some very rare days I would receive ten Pfennigs as a four-or-five-year-old to walk to the mom-and-pop grocery store in our street to figure how much I could get with it.

Breakfast was German rye bread (by the way, not the American version with caraway seeds that is sold as German) with a spread of butter and home-made jam and a cup or two of hot cocoa. Fridays, my mother baked cake for the weekend. Every once in a while, we had German pancakes, crêpes a little thicker than the French variety, spread with sugar and with a compote on the side. And when we went out – which only happened very rarely – one glass of sweet soda was pretty much the limit (free refills were unheard of in European gastronomy). That was pretty much all the sugar my mother would permit us children to have. Apart from all the seasonal fresh fruit we ate.

Coming to the US my very first time as a teenager, I was thrown by the variety of sugared cereals that each and every household seemed to keep around – even with colorful marshmallows, oh my! As a teenager, I enjoyed it, of course. Today, I keep it to oatmeal and yoghurt again, maybe with a spoon of jam or some fresh fruit. Rather a savory open sandwich, though. But sugary cereal for me is simply ... too sweet. I guess that my body was given an imprint in my childhood as to how much sweetness it can stand. And it isn't very much. You will find that a lot of Mid and Northern European visitors and/or immigrants of my generation feel the same way.

These days, as places in the US raise a tax on sugared sodas to whatever purpose they claim, I still find that a whole lot of sweetness is added to food items that for a German are quite unexpected. Just take a look at bread labels and see how much sugar or corn syrup is added to this staple. And I have had sandwiches where I simply winced about the bread's sweet flavor – it doesn't work for me at all, especially not when eating some savory topping. And, of course, there are the very obvious items as well: honey-glazed ham, maple syrup infused bacon, candied cranberries in salads, thick layers of icing on cakes. I instinctively abstain from these.

I sometimes wonder whether these are remainders of early pioneer day preservation methods, when salt was probably quite rare, but sugar – as in honey or maple syrup – available. For obvious reasons, pioneers would have to have traded for imported salt before greater resources became available through salt mines, Syracuse in New York probably being the oldest. You can only start mining once you are safely settled. In Europe, that tradition goes back to the medieval ages. Salt was that widely used for preservation that it actually is still reflected in the Swabian word "Gesälz" (pronounce guh-'zells), meaning "salted" and signifying jams. Originally it described anything salted down – interestingly it stuck with the least likely to have ever been preserved with salt: fruit!

Whether it is a matter of what we have gotten used to over the centuries, whether adding corn syrup to as many items as possible is in order to support the corn industry, or whether it is just a matter of very individual taste – I find it interesting, because the consumption of sugar in the US is simply striking compared to where I come from. And it is quite hard to evade eating it, unless you check each and every label for the contents.

I have started baking my own bread every once in a while. The German bakery here in Lakewood uses original recipes from overseas, too. Every once in a while, I buy American bread to console my husband's American taste buds. He compromises on my weird tastes a lot, too, as it is. I admit to having baked cupcakes and topped them with icing in the past. I won't pull a face or get picky when I am invited and there is sugary food on the table. But you will never find Ambrosia with marshmallows or Jell-O coming out of my kitchen. My taste buds seem to have made enough sweet memories back when – even with only one piece of candy a day.

White Asparagus

What is it with German-Americans and their love for white asparagus? We keep craving it especially during spring time. We do a dance of joy as soon as we spot some in a supermarket. We talk about it on Facebook when we have found some, and all our German-American friends go "OMG, where?! Got to get some!" Whereas most of my American friends wonder what white asparagus is, what you do with it, and how it tastes.

I grew up with a German adage that went along the lines that if you wanted to be highly esteemed, you'd have to make yourself rare. Maybe that is one of the secrets of white asparagus. You don't get it all year long. Its season in Europe is limited from March (in the Mediterranean areas) to early June, whereas green asparagus is available all year long. German white asparagus is harvested only from mid-April through early June. And trust me, it's a delicacy.

But what lends it such status? First of all, not every kind of soil is suitable for growing white asparagus. It needs to be rich and sandy at the same time, making regions like the Rhine valley perfect growing lands. Only the subterranean sprouts are harvested. That's why the stems stay white, sometimes with a touch of purple to their tips, whereas green asparagus has grown out of the earth. You may have guessed already – white asparagus is way juicier and tenderer than its full-grown green version.

Romans had introduced white asparagus to Germania, but with their return to Italy the knowledge of the veggie became extinct. Only in the 16th century white asparagus was rediscovered. A vegetable that grew only in specific areas and was harvested from underground, stem by stem with a knife – such hard-gained produce had to be a dish on aristocratic and very rich people's tables only. Even today white asparagus has its price – a decimal pound of the German variety can cost up to 12 dollars at the beginning of the season. The white asparagus we sometimes find here in Western Washington is mostly from Peru, it seems, and not as tender and juicy as what I am used to. But it is not as pricey either and flavor-wise still the real deal.

These days, Germany is white asparagus crazy. There are entire white asparagus menus at restaurants. It usually gets served by the decimal pound. People buy it by the kilogram on farmers markets, in supermarkets, fresh from the farm. There are countless white asparagus recipes on websites on the internet. And I have found myself checking the produce sections of farmers markets and supermarkets over here for the white delicacy as well – so far in vain.

So, how do you prep these stems? Cut off the cut ends by half an inch or more. You don't want the dry, maybe woodsy ends on your plate. Then you use a knife or potato peeler to carefully and thinly shave the stems. It doesn't matter whether you cook the stems in one piece or cut them up so they fit into your pot. I usually put in a quarter stick of butter per pound and sprinkle the asparagus with a tad of sugar and a tad of salt. I also like to add a bit of tarragon to the dish. Add some water so the asparagus doesn't burn. Then stew gently for five to ten minutes, depending on the thickness of the stems. Boiled jacked potatoes make a perfect companion for white asparagus. And then just let your imagination roll. Have it the vegetarian way – it's perfect. Add a few slices of ham – great. Sauce Hollandaise? A classic. Add Schnitzel or salmon – you will be delighted, too.

As to the peels and ends, you can create a fantastic broth from them. Just simmer them in a bit of salted water, then sieve the broth into a different pot. Bind the broth with a bit of flour or potato starch dissolved in cold water and add a bit of sour cream. Season with a pinch of butter, pepper, and ground nutmeg. Asparagus cream soup is a delicious appetizer. And that way you have made use of the peels as well. No waste, no want.

Ah, white asparagus ... I wonder why it seemingly isn't grown on local farms in Western Washington. Maybe we don't have the soil to do so. Maybe it's simply not known to farmers well enough. I'm pretty sure that German-Americans would rip the good stuff out of their hands ... Well, maybe next year?

Kaffeeklatsch

The German term "Kaffeeklatsch" (pronounce 'kuffah-klutsh, meaning gossiping over coffee) has made it into the American language. It is usually a thing of the afternoon hours, and it's something you enjoy at a private home as well as at a café. Unfortunately, the classic café is becoming more and more a thing of the past in my mother country. There are still a few of the Vienna-style coffeehouses in Germany, but the slightly baroque interior, the quiet classic music, and the typical German Torte with whipped cream or buttercream seem to be replaced more and more with a mix of French bistro and Western Washingtonian coffee chain culture.

A kaffeeklatsch is pretty much the daytime counterpart to the originally male-only, rather alcoholic "Stammtisch" (pronounce 'Shtum-tish, literally meaning a table for regulars, but also a regular meeting) taking place in taverns. Who knows when the kaffeeklatsch even developed?! It might have been born out of boredom – it certainly was something that only the well-off and idle could afford in the beginning. Times have changed. Cake and torte have become widely affordable; and it is often young mothers who create a kaffeeklatsch for other peers in connection with a playdate for their kids. And then, of course, there are the big occasions like weddings, baptisms, confirmation/first communion, birthdays, and funerals where coffee and cake are at the center of the rituals. The festivity of making time for leisure is simply underlined by fancy cakes and a cup of coffee … as well as the gossip.

The working world and younger generations have turned the culture of kaffeeklatsch a bit around in my mother country. A coffee is often grabbed on the go. Calorie counting has replaced the indulgence of whipped cream torte and buttercream creations (except on occasions as mentioned above). And due to sparse leisure during daytime, the Stammtisch has become the more obvious alternative for working men and women, often enough separate according to gender. (Girls simply can discuss girl stuff better when there is no man who rolls their eyes at them, right? And I guess the same goes for men vice versa.)

To my surprise, Western Washington seems to gain more of a café culture these days than my mother country manages to obtain. And it is not just the older generation who seem to indulge in it.

The first time I entered a café over here was in Olympia. It was a well-known German café with a large cake display, and I had a craving for Bienenstich (pronounce 'Bee-nan-shtih, meaning bee sting, a cake filled with vanilla buttercream and topped with a baked layer of almonds and honey). If you grow up with German cake you know what it has to taste like – let's say the cake the pastry chefs sold me that day was perfection, and I grew very nostalgic over the slice, while I was chewing. Lakewood has its own German pastry shop, and there is often a queue at the cake counter, while in the back you hear Germans (mostly ladies) chatting in their mother tongue. There is also some wonderful selection of cakes and torte at Lakewood's Polish & German restaurant.

Well, it was a surprise to me that there are German coffee places over here at all. The only cake I had experienced in the US so far were those sponge cake & icing creations for dessert after a festive dinner. And – to be honest – I'm not a fan of most of these cakes or of stuffing a dessert after an already opulent meal.

No, the biggest surprise is how many cake studios and cafés have been springing up over the past eight years that I have had the pleasure to live here. Because they are celebrating the art of making dessert in the most eclectic ways imaginable. They have the charm of classic European cafés without being stuffy or baroque. They have cake displays that make even a philistine as me wonder how this or that concoction might taste. Or how the decoration can ever be created in such a delicate way. And whether a trip to a specific dessert maker up north in Bellingham might be worth the gas mileage or should better be connected with something that justifies the mere consumption of mouth-drooling caloric bliss.

Meanwhile, I look at my recipe books and skip all the pages that relate to baking cakes. And I wonder how my mother managed to bake weekend cakes and torte for her entire life and gave our family a daily kaffeeklatsch without us bursting from our seams. Ah, her wonderful creations … Maybe I should work on my baking skills a bit more consistently. Though – do I really want more extra-pounds on my hips?

Cabbage and Taters

I have been called some names over here after my arrival. One of them was "sauerkraut" or "Kraut". There is worse you could be called - still ...

Actually, I like sauerkraut. When I was a child, my mother always gave me some fresh from the can, and as a grown-up I still sometimes indulge in a tiny can of Mildessa kraut every once in a while.

Why is kraut such a popular dish in Germany? And why do we eat it sour so very often? That is an easy one. Sour cabbage keeps, as the acidity serves as a preservative. And because sour cabbage of any kind helps break the fat of anything eaten along with it. That is why we have sauerkraut with fat pork dishes such as hocks, sausages, or a crisp roast with a thick crust on. That is why we have hot red sour cabbage with goose or other poultry.

The area I come from in Germany is famous for its coned white cabbages. There are even festivals celebrating the cabbage harvest. But there are many more kinds of cabbages in my mother country, and interestingly enough they have different names and sometimes even flavors from those over here. The green cabbage here would probably still count as white cabbage over there. But German "green cabbage" isn't even to be found over here in Western Washington. At least I haven't found it so far. There is kale – Germans sometimes think it's the same as Gruenkohl (pronounce: 'groon-coal, meaning green cabbage), but it consists of separate leaves here,

193

whereas it would be a head over there, and American kale tastes like kohlrabi greens, not like Gruenkohl. Savoy cabbage here is pretty much what Wirsing is over in Germany. It lends itself marvelously for cabbage rolls stuffed with ground meat, but it stands in its own right when prepared as a side dish. And there are a lot more kinds besides – you get the picture.

Did I say that Germans would never serve more than one kind of cabbage side with an entrée? Next time you go for a German restaurant experience, keep in mind that the combo of sauerkraut, cold (!) red cabbage and "German" potato salad is typical American. You would never serve the three alongside each other overseas, just as you don't have a roulade on the same plate as a schnitzel or pork roast. Germans are pretty puristic that way.

Now, why did I put German potato salad into inverted commas? Because there is no such thing. What is sold as "German" potato salad over here is one with mayonnaise. That is one regional variety. I come from an area where it is usually made with a mix of broth and vinaigrette, eaten lukewarm. My mother made hers from cold jacket potatoes with a vinaigrette. Some people add bacon bits into their salads. My mother used veggies like cucumber slices or bell pepper cubes, chopped Belgian endive or chicory to add some crunch. Or cubed pickles. When we had potato salad, it served as a stand-in for a potato/starchy side as well as a salad/veggie side. We had it along with sausages, Schnitzel, or fried fish. No additional sides needed.

There are probably as many potato salad recipes in Germany as there are households. Maybe even more if you count the variety of ingredients. I use my late mother's five different recipe variants, my mother-in-law's recipe, and two variants of my own. And if you'd like to try something different from the boxed potato salad from your supermarket, try this link for a change: https://germangirlinamerica.com/german-style-potato-salad-recipes/. These are recipes collected from Germans – and they might encourage you to think outside the box. There goes German potato salad for you!

Salt-water boiled peeled potatoes, jacket potatoes, potato cakes (similar to hash brown patties, but thinner and including onions), pan-fried potatoes, potato dumplings, mashed potatoes – these are equally classic German potato sides but occurring less frequently on any menu over here. If you run into them (and they are usually not called "German") – try them! Because these are as authentic as any potato salad.

Did I serve pan-fried potato wedges and some beautifully duck-fat and wine-infused savoy cabbage as sides for a Schnitzel only the other day? Ah, cabbage and taters – so simple, so versatile, and so traditionally German!

Ice Cream

Hot summer days in my German 70s childhood are connected with the taste of juicy, tangy peaches and – ice cream. I will never forget the cold strawberry taste on Sunday afternoons when my parents took my brother and me for walks, usually dipping into a tiny corner pub just to buy popsicles. What bliss to get one of those 25-Pfennig-delicacies! Or the fun of making popsicles at home, pouring orange juice into molds and freezing them. I remember bugging my mom for hours about when they would be ready – and the joy of sucking the cold sweetness out of the fragile ice block, while my little hands were turning all sticky.

Later, I spent some of my pocket money on popsicles called Capri, or Miami, or Dolomiti, all of them sorbets. Until I stopped having popsicles at all and fell for ice coffee (the German kind with vanilla ice cream and whipped cream). In the end, I stopped eating ice cream almost at all, but enjoyed a few binges of eating up to eight gelateria-sized scoops of all different kinds of colors and flavors at one time. Boy, I was cold after that!

Funny enough, I never thought I'd ever run an ice cream place myself one day. Or better – an ice cream social. I guess, ice cream socials are a specifically American thing, and mine was at the 4th July at the start of my second year after I came over here. Actually, I was quite surprised when the Steilacoom Historical Museum director – with whom I was working as an office manager and docent at the time – asked me to chair the event. I was flattered big-time. An immigrant chairing one of *the* museum events on *the* national holiday?! I also was scared big-time. What if I messed up?

I started out with creating to-do-lists with a time line. I got myself a food worker license for Washington State. Then I called in my board, among them a very cheerful lady who turned out to be super-efficient and also the one who would keep smiling through the toughest of heat and business on *the* day. We had about three meetings resulting in more lists. We went doing groceries and storing away things in the museum's freezers. I made dozens of phone calls to people who had signed up to help with the ice cream social and would show, to people who had signed up only to withdraw, and to people I knew but who hadn't signed up and were game. At nights I felt butterflies in my tummy growing to the size of dolphins, almost making me sick by the time 4th July actually arrived.

I woke to a cloudless day, the hottest of that whole year. I grabbed some last-minute-requisites, and off I went through our sleepy small-town that was just slowly waking up. The newly re-opened corner café at one of the main crossings had already set out their garden furniture and put up umbrellas, the pub people across were setting up a stage and long beer tables; further on the non-denominational church people were setting up their decoration. All of a sudden, I felt so much more part of this national holiday!

Long story short: We had the best 4th July Ice Cream Social in the museum's history by then. Not only did it stay hot.

The patio with its tent, chairs, and tables was crowded with people. Even the museum's lawn became part of the event. People showed up in fancy costumes – one lady was dressed up as Lady Liberty herself! There were lines around the block, even though my ice cream teams were selling tickets, scraping scoops, decorating sundaes, and filling up root beer floats as if their life counted upon it. All day long more people showed up to volunteer if needed, people I knew I could rely on. The parade went past the museum, and I could only catch glimpses from my point of coordination. I was bustling around the grounds for ten hours without realizing it. Not a single health inspector showed up, but – oh! – my teams were adamant about keeping up standards. And we were clean sold out of ice cream and root beer half an hour before closing time.

Only hours later – after I had helped clean up, done the books, cooked dinner, and walked down to the harbor to watch the fireworks – did I find that I had missed out on one essential thing that Independence Day. In the glory of rockets bursting in air and coloring the smooth water in the Sound with their brilliant reflection, I realized I had not had a single scoop of ice cream myself!

Corn

The first time I had corn was sometime in the 70s – from a jar of mixed pickles. I loved it. It was about the same time when, as seven-year-olds, we kids of the neighborhood broke into a farmer's corn field and helped us to raw corn on the cob. I loved that, too. You didn't find fresh corn in German supermarkets back then. I'm not even sure whether the concept of popcorn had made it to German movie theaters and fairs before the 1970s. Germans simply didn't eat it. It became popular only with and for my generation. And that was for a reason.

Maybe you know some Germans of the generation that grew up during World War II. Ask them whether they like eating corn. If they say "no", it is pretty symptomatic. Corn used to be exclusively cattle and pig food in Germany. Germans grew up on rye and wheat, on barley and oats.

World War II had pretty much turned Germany into a ground zero. People had no homes, and the crops were lost. Potato beetle plagues and harsh weather (both scorching summers and icy winters) made the first years after the war a matter of survival. If it hadn't been for international charities and Hoover meals, millions would have starved to death.

This was about the time that corn was introduced into the German food plan. Legend has it that the Germans (who exactly?!) were asked (by whom?!) what they needed most (everything!), and that a translator botched the German word "Korn", i.e. grain, and translated it as "corn". So, corn was imported big time, and all of a sudden, Germans were dealing with a diet so much sweeter than anything they were used to: corn flour, corn meal, cornbread. There was no butter on the cobs or jam to go with a corn cake. Maybe some felt it was adding insult to injury being given "pig food". Be it as it is – even if you were fed your favorite dish 365 days a year for seemingly endless years (my guess is that the corn diet vanished after the first better crops), you would have developed kind of a disgust even with that favorite dish. You would not ever want to taste it again. How so much more with food that goes against your grain?! If somebody served it to you even in the best of times, you'd think of the worst place you'd been in your life: when you were utterly helpless and vulnerable. This is why some of your German friends born before 1945 might not be into corn on the cob, corn muffins, corn bread, corn anything.

I hadn't been aware of this as a child. Therefore, when on my first US vacation as a teenager I tasted my first corn on the cob, buttered up and seasoned with salt and pepper, I returned home with raving reviews and the wish to try this in my family. That was when I first heard about my father's corn aversion. When my brother returned from his first US vacation two years later, he was totally in love with corn on the cob as well. We got our fill of canned corn after the Ukrainian nuclear catastrophe in Chernobyl in 1986. My mother didn't buy any fresh produce that year or the next for fear of feeding her family highly contaminated dishes. I still love the corn and kidney bean salad with an onion vinaigrette, which was one of our main sides during those two years. It was changed up cleverly and by far not the only canned vegetable we ate.

Today, I create anything vegetable with corn. I'm not keen on the sweet flavor in corn cakes and corn bread at all, though. Maybe that is my German food heritage – what is ingrained in my genes. My husband and I even planted corn in a raised bed this spring, and now we are waiting anxiously whether the high stalks of painted corn will, finally, turn out some cobs.

I am grateful that there was never a day in my life when something that I might have loved was turned into something I had to eat because I would have starved otherwise. I'm grateful that I never had to eat anything I hated for years in a row. I'm grateful that I was never, at any time in my life, at a point when I'd been starving, period. But whenever I eat corn on the cob, I think of these family members and friends of mine who survived a catastrophe because of this incredibly versatile plant.

Squash

If anybody had ever told me twenty-five years ago that I'd become a fervent squash lover and couldn't wait for a specific kind to appear in the markets every fall, I'd have laughed in their faces. Because Germans don't differentiate between pumpkin and squash, but use the term "Kuerbis" (pronounce curr-biss, i.e. pumpkin) for either. I thought all must be tasting pretty much the same. And as my very first encounter with them was of the sweet-sour pickled variety, which four-year-old me totally disliked, I kept just admiring the *look* of the plants per se.

The big change came during my business life when I had my very first taste of a "pumpkin soup" (which I strongly suspect was made from squash), topped with a dollop of whipped cream and toasted pumpkin seeds. I needed to replicate this dish. I knew a colleague of mine had a recipe – and she introduced me to the Uchiki Kuri. As it is one of the most common winter squashes to come across in Germany, I had no trouble finding one. And then I started experimenting.

Change to overseas. The first fall I was over here, I kept looking in vain for any Uchiki Kuri. I hunted supermarkets high and low – nothing. I found butternut and Blue Hubbard, spaghetti squash and sugar pumpkins, but none of my beloved Hokkaido kind. I was disappointed. I had expected them to be abundant in a region with so many Asian residents. But then – maybe Hokkaido squash didn't belong to the Asian cuisine at all?

I kept looking the following year. And then, the year after, I found some at a supermarket in Lakewood Towne Center. I must have been beaming all over the face during my entire shopping spree that day. I bought not just one, I bought three just to make sure that my fall was going to be perfect on the culinary side. I also bought some decorative squash, just because the find of my edible favorite ones had made me so happy.

My search was on anew when the same supermarket left Towne Center and with it so many culinary options that others nearby simply don't offer. It was disheartening. Even more so since few sales people had ever heard of the squash by either of its three names. Not even the pumpkin/squash farms around here sold any on their premises. Instead I bought a few other kinds of winter squash. I came to fairly like butternut and Delicata, but never became a friend of carnival or turban squash. That same year, I came across Uchiki Kuri only in a regional supermarket in Seattle.

These days, I drive up to a certain supermarket in Proctor or one in University Place to get my fill of Hokkaido squash in fall. And then I prepare near a gallon of squash puree to freeze. And I roast slices of it just with olive oil, a few herbs, salt, and pepper. And I make soup. As you can eat the bright red skin of the Kuri squash, the dish gains an intense orange color. Adding some chicken bouillon, white wine, a dollop of sour cream, and chopped pistachios is my kitchen hack. And you bet that this soup has become a family favorite and a fall staple at our home ever since.

Ah, fall and winter squash are coming soon! I will go "hunt" for my beautiful Uchiki Kuri again. Sure, I will enjoy some butternut and spaghetti squash along the way, too. I will love looking at squash and pumpkins at farm stores or driving by the colorful fields between here and Mt. Rainier. Because fall gains color with these beautiful, versatile gourds. I cannot imagine fall without decorative squash at my home anymore. Or without a carved pumpkin by the front door. But to me the best of all will always be that one evasive kind that was so easy to come by in my German past and seems to be such an uncommon species over here. – If you come across them anywhere, do yourselves a favor and give them a try!

Christstollen

These days, stores in the area which have been carrying German Christmas treats are pretty much sold out. One of the most traditional baked goods – and I have to admit definitely not my favorite one – is Christstollen (pronounce: 'kreest-shtoll-lan). But that's because I'm not one for sweet yeast doughs at all. So why write an article about it? Because it is such a tradition and the story behind it is quite exquisite.

Christstollen is a typical fasting dish originally containing only yeast, flour, oil, and water. It is heavy; it is shaped like a log; which is why they may have called it "Stollen" in Germany in the first place. The word derives etymologically from a word for post or stanchion. And its taste must have been horribly bland when it was invented. Still, it became a staple during advent time in the 1400s.

The ingredients for it sound common enough. But indeed, oil was rather hard to come by in some regions, and in the German dukedom of Saxony oil was more expensive and scarcer than butter. But butter is certainly not a Lenten item. Which made the Duke of Saxony appeal to the Pope to let Saxon bakers use butter for the Stollen instead of oil. The first of these requests was denied in 1450. Five popes and four decades later, a wiser pope saw a moneymaker in the appeal and granted the use of butter in 1490, but demanded an annual tax from the bakers, which was supposed to help build a church. I almost suspect this tax helped further the cause of Protestantism instead. It became obsolete when Saxony turned Lutheran. And butter stayed one of the basic ingredients of the Stollen.

Today, we find all kinds of Christstollen enriched with candied fruit, rum, marzipan, spices, raisins, and/or almonds. The heavy log is brushed with butter and covered with confectioners' sugar. The most famous Stollen, also renowned as Striezel (pronounce: 'shtreet-sal), comes from the German city of Dresden where even the Christmas market has been named for it. It is exported to countries all around the globe, and if you check your local supermarkets and German delis, you might still be lucky to find some.

Many German households pride themselves on baking these loaves themselves. Usually, they are stored away weeks before they are consumed. This never worked in my family; fresh from the oven Stollen was loved so well, it was usually devoured within a week. My mother usually ended up baking Christstollen until Twelfth Night because it was so coveted. Not by me, as noted before, but I always had a courtesy slice to get into the right advent mood. After that I gladly nibbled on Lebkuchen (pronounce: 'lahp-coo-hen, a kind of gingerbread) or other typical delicacies of a less Lenten character.

You are right in presuming I haven't continued the tradition of baking Christstollen in my own household ever. Still, when I see the first Christstollen pop up on the shelves in local stores, I feel that old nostalgia swipe over me. And I am almost tempted to buy myself just one of the tinier loaves … Almost.

Odds and Ends

Friends

Emigration means cutting off a lot of roots. It disrupts your job and deeply affects your family and friends. The change from having a social life in your old surroundings to having none at all in your new ones, at first, is a natural given. But it also is a chance to shed people who haven't been great friends in the past and even to welcome people whom you thought to have lost back into your life. It's a tumultuous situation for all sides.

At first, my emigration made a wave of people back in Germany gravitate towards me because they were simply curious about my new chapter in life. Maybe they were indulging some distant hope for a gratis vacation in the US someday. Well, none of these oh so suddenly interested people stayed in contact with me for longer than half a year after I left. It was obviously way too tedious for them to keep writing emails or letters. And once my way of life changed from a professional career to one of volunteering, home-making, and writing novels, they lost interest entirely.

I also lost some of my former long-time friends. In their eyes I had changed so entirely they didn't understand me any longer. Probably, they hadn't ever listened or believed me when I told them I was simply happy with where life was placing me. All of a sudden, this formerly single woman was centering her life on a partner who had become her husband. I was going to leave behind my career, I was walking out on them, and the journey was to be on a one-way ticket to a place far away! They weren't at the center of my plans anymore – how very selfish of me! Those people dropped out mostly on a bitter note.

But I also kept a whole lot of my old friends. Thanks to the internet, we still keep contact in real time even though half a world apart. Social media have kept me in touch with some of my oldest friends, while bringing me a load of entirely new ones. They simply accept who I am, and I know and hope one or the other will come over someday. Actually, a few of them already did – to make sure that I'm fine, to surprise me, to celebrate with me.

But what about friends over here? When I started out at my new home and in my new life, hardly anybody was aware of my arrival. My husband had been working night shifts until I joined him. Therefore, barely anybody knew us in our little town. If I didn't want to mold in isolation, we had to reach out ourselves.

It is true that opportunity drops into your lap when you least expect it. For me, it came in the shape of a door hanger by our local museum association, and I grasped it. We signed up as members and as volunteers. And lo and behold! – my lonesome days were over. Another couple of weeks later, I was invited to join a museum committee, and from there it went like wildfire. I became a docent, staff at the annual Apple Squeeze, helped at a baking party, sang with a caroling group – you name it. One tiny step started an avalanche of events and meeting new people. After not even half a year, people in town started to recognize me, to chat with me across their garden fences, to invite me into their homes, to tell me stories about their past and town history. My new lifestyle – so far removed from my former one – has been permitting me to go and meet people on an entirely private, non-career-based, and personal basis.

It has been almost nine years now since I first set foot in the Pacific Northwest, and I've made an astonishing number of wonderful friendships and acquaintances. Social media even connect some of my old friends with my new ones, though, most likely, they will never meet. It takes a while to make new friends, of course. It doesn't matter whether you just move to a different town in your own mother country or, as an immigrant, to an entirely different world. I love the thought that, one day, all these new friendships will be old ones, too. And that the place that sometimes is still kind of new has already become another home.

Homesickness

"Aren't you homesick? What about Germany do you miss most?"

These are probably the questions I've been asked most often after coming over here. And I almost feel like a traitor when I reply "No" and "Nothing". In the age of lightfast communication and worldwide import/exports, with a bit of imagination and improvisation, you can pretend to be anywhere anytime if you care to do so. I am simply happy where I am.

People keep telling me about German restaurants in the area – it's probably a very exotic and nice experience for them. But as to me – I know how to cook authentic German-style, and, apart from this, I am also a very experimental cook. So, I'm not yearning to go out for Schnitzel. I got it here, right at home, whenever I want to fry one.

Maybe I miss the more than 1,500 kinds of German cold cuts and the more than 300 kinds of German breads, though I'm lucky to live almost around the corner from a wonderful German deli that offers quite an array of both. I just wish there was more variety more widely spread. The cold cut counter in a German corner store or at a butcher's offers more kinds of cold cuts within half a square yard than most of the aisles of a US supermarket, I'm afraid. And the over-sweetened and spongey quality of most American breads is still undelightful to my German palate. But I also have to say that it has changed quite a bit since my arrival seven years ago, and the variety on bread shelves and in meat counters over here is growing.

Apart from that – I have long got used to working with a washer with a spindle inside instead of a tumbling drum. I found a European style vacuum cleaner that I don't have to clean out and end up dustier myself than its insides. I have learned to bend plugs so they don't fall out of their sockets. And I have adjusted to the Washington outdoor lifestyle and discarded most of my high heels from my former German city life in the favor of sneakers and flip-flops.

What do I miss? Would *you* be homesick in Paradise?

I came here out of love and very much of my own free will, ready to stay here for the rest of my life by the side of my wonderful husband. I lack nothing, and the older I get, the more basic and abstract my needs and wants are becoming. Apart from Western Washington's coverage of all creature comforts, the state offers the most astonishing variety in Nature what with prairies, Alpine mountains, islands, and National Parks. There are cultural events in abundance – you only have to choose. There are public libraries for soul and brain food – and you don't even have to pay for this service unlike in Germany.

So many people here say they love Germany as soon as they hear that this is my mother country. They start telling me about their wonderful experiences over there. They even start speaking German with me. But now it's *my* turn to experience *your* country. I let myself go for it with all my senses. Each and every day, I end up overwhelmed with happiness. I find that people around here (contrary to the clichés about Western Washingtonians) are welcoming, warm-hearted, and open-minded. They are dedicated to all kinds of wonderful volunteering. They are aware of and appreciate the amazing landscape they are living in.

Clichés have it that when Germans adjusts, they do it by 150 percent. Maybe it's because so many Germans generally do anything they do with a 150-%-dedication. It's what made us to be one of the leading economic powers in Europe. It's what made us a "nation of poets and thinkers", a nation of inventors. It's what made us the world champions in traveling. It has also turned us a nation with one of the highest emigration rates in Europe in the past two decades – maybe because we keep thinking opportunity is better by 150 percent elsewhere.

Just let me make my point again: I came to the US for love, not for having too little opportunity where I was born, grew up, and lived for almost 42 years. No, I am not homesick. No, I miss nothing. And yes, I'm committed by a 150 percent never to let it come that far.

Chimes

The other day, my husband and I happened across a Russian food and crafts bazaar in an orthodox Cathedral in Seattle. Over a bowl of delicious borsht and a steaming pirogue filled with spicy beef I suddenly choked. There was distinct chiming overhead, not of one, no, of various church bells. To a European like me this is a sound from home.

Basically, I cannot imagine Germany without the daily sound of bells. Town halls over there have bells, too, but most of them play folksongs and other worldly pieces (and to my ears they mostly sound painfully out of tune). Church bells are something totally different – and they were pretty much the first thing I missed when coming over here.

Sundays here are business as usual sound-wise. Over in Germany, they are special. Most German cities, except spa towns, have strict opening and closing times for businesses. Sundays are very, very quiet, as almost everything is closed. Noisy activities such as lawn mowing are prohibited. Even agriculture usually tries to keep Sunday rest, unless they have to work to not endanger the harvest. Therefore, imagine the impact of even as much as a single church bell! Half an hour before church service, you hear the chapel call usually performed by a smaller force of bells in the belfries. Five minutes before the beginning of service, you will be able to hear the full peal of bells. And not just of one church. But of all the surrounding churches that start their services at the same time. It's a feast of rich sounds, not like the Big Ben peal, but something way more insisting. A single bell always starts tolling after the very first line of the Lord's Prayer during church service.

I used to live in hearing distance of neighborhood churches for almost all of my life. It never disturbed me. Neither did the quarter-hourly and hourly clock chimes that are a tradition transmitted from the Medieval Ages (back then, the bells also served as an alarm for fire, pest, or impeding war). After a while, you simply get so used to bell chimes you don't even hear them anymore. But you miss them immediately once they are under repair.

German farmers markets are often started on the chime of a bell, and they close on its sound some hours later. Noon is marked by a full peal – originally the lunch break hour for farm and trade workers. You know when somebody has a memorial service at the cemetery that day, as the funeral bell tolls in the morning. Saturday afternoon chiming means that somebody is getting married at that church. Prayer bells at six in the evening were the sign for kids to go home for dinner in past days (I have my doubts they are that still). Saturday evening full peals welcome in Sunday.

Church bells have been subdividing European lives for centuries. They have been used for messages, celebrations, warning, and mourning. Most Germans today might not even be aware of their meaning anymore, as our world gets more and more secular and/or multi-cultural. Church bells have secular as well as religious purposes.

One of the most touching and almost overwhelming moments, by the way, is always right at midnight of New Year's Eve. After the hourly chime, each and every bell of each and every chapel, church, and cathedral all across the nation suddenly bursts into an incredibly joyful and celebratory peal to greet the New Year. It doesn't matter whether you interpret this as a worldly or as a religious symbol.

When I heard the silvery peal of the bells of Saint Spiridon Orthodox Cathedral in Seattle that afternoon, it felt like a greeting from my past. For a moment I stopped chewing and just listened. Then the clinking of spoons against china bowls and the humming of quiet conversation drowned them out again. The moment was over. But the memory still reverberates.

Changing Homes

Getting married is easy, staying married is work. That's at least what a whole lot of people perceive it to be. Let me tell you – even *getting* married is not always easy, especially when you are marrying someone of a different nationality and intend to assume that nationality yourself. Almost nine years ago, native German I was going to marry a US citizen outside his country; not even in the country he was working in at that time, but on my own turf.

Ah, romance! I had finally found my knight of shining armor after two decades of neighbors, friends, and great-aunts asking: "Don't you want to get married?" And here, at the threshold of almost forty, I finally announced what probably nobody would have expected anymore: "I'm engaged to get married." Certainly, that was the easiest part. It was the romance, fun, and goose-bumps part. What came then was a dive into a jungle of forms to fill in and actions to take.

My official life by the side of my American future-husband started soon after the announcement. I had no idea that my future-husband's commander had to sign a paper permitting my fiancé to marry me. Had I known then, I'd probably have sat tied in knots at the ball I was introduced to him.

It was only the beginning of the paperwork. After US medical checks and that marriage permit, I found out about the German side of the paper war. Had I imagined it would be easy? It took us three months to get all my husband's papers from the USA – and only then would the registrar in my little home town file us for a marriage date. Which was to be just a month before my husband would have to return to the United States. Meanwhile we started work on all the forms we needed to file for a spouse's visa for me.

Our wedding day was perfection. I'd even managed to obtain two pastors, one German, one American, to perform the church ceremony after a bi-lingual registrar's ceremony. But the jungle of formalities left us only this short breather.

We were to fill in forms, wait for more instructions, wait for another step forward for exactly a year. We were living apart by then, my husband here in Washington State, I still with my job at a publishing house in Southern Germany. We called each other on the phone daily. There were times when we were "on the road", and we had to rearrange our phone schedule. It was a time of romance and of fighting impatience. I was not permitted to visit him in the US; he made it to Germany only for a few days over Christmas. That was our first year of marriage.

I got my visa on our first wedding anniversary. It was not an indisputable triumph. It meant organizing my move, and the total cancellation of my former existence. It was stressful, bitter-sweet, harrowing, exhilarating, surreal.

Whom do I remember best in my fight with the forms? The US consular in Frankfurt who winked at me and said "You'll be fine" though she was not supposed to tell me the outcome of my visa interview right away? The immigration officer who called my name from an upper gallery at SeaTac

Airport to toss me some paperwork to the downstairs baggage retrieval, as he'd forgotten to hand it to me a couple of minutes before at the point of no return? The smile of the custom's officer "*You're* fine", after he had sent everybody in front of me to unpack their luggage, but waiving me through?

What I remember best is the helpfulness of all the administrative people, be they German or American. They are usually feared. They are reputed to be stern and unfriendly. They are not. They are as friendly as you approach them. They are helpful as soon as you let on about your helplessness. They share a smile, they crack jokes. They even send paperwork flying, if that's the way to help the process.

I finally reached my husband's arms after a tough year's separation. We had met quite a few wonderful people along that hard path in places we didn't expect them. Today, we share memories of comforting and encouraging each other, which makes us stick together even better.

Trolley Trips

"Where would you want our new home to be?" my husband asked me over the phone. We'd been separated by his reposting to the United States, and I was still in Germany waiting for my visa. I had the anticipation I wouldn't hold a job immediately after arriving in the US. And I wouldn't need a car, then, just for my weekly groceries. I was dead-sure about that.

"Well," I decided, "Either near a supermarket or on a bus route."

"Which would you rather have?"

"The bus route, as it makes me more flexible."

I finally made it to the US almost a year after that call. My husband had found a nice house near a bus route. The bus stations were located near enough downhill, but I knew it would be still an uphill trip with my groceries. When I first ventured out, I did so with some cotton bags and a backpack. A bit later in the day, I dragged myself uphill, loaded with groceries, and I felt as if my arms were pulled out of their sockets.

Almost two months after my arrival, my moving container got delivered and along with it a wedding gift that would make shopping so much easier: a sparkling new device that my brother had called "the Porsche in shopping trolleys". It came with big rubber tires and a blue waterproof cloth container. Even a frozen goods compartment was incorporated in the design. This was the latest model available in Germany obviously – and quite conspicuous at that.

221

Hauling the thing on the bus was easy enough. But once on the bus I found it difficult to find room for it. Either it got stuck in the aisle with one of its wheels or I had to sit in the seats reserved for the disabled. Its width alone made it impossible to roll it through the aisle, so I had to lift it to get into the more spacious back. With the groceries inside that was impossible.

Of course, the design of the trolley made for plenty of conversation. Everybody asked me where I'd got it from. And from there it was only a short cut to talking about shopping opportunities, Germany, the beauties of the surroundings, the weather, you name it. Many also took the trolley for a chic suitcase. They must have wondered what I was doing, pulling it into stores.

It struck me then that shopping trolleys over here are mostly collapsible wire constructions, rigid and see-through, rather practical than a statement of fashion. They are made for taking on the bus, for being folded up to go in front of your knees in a seat row if need be.

Finally, my husband and I figured a way for me to go to the stores later in the afternoons, so he could pick me up after work. In my favorite supermarket – now sadly gone and with it a lot of neighborly friendliness – you had to deposit shopping bags, rucksacks, or trolleys at the front desk, while doing groceries. For sure, that big, bright-blue trolley was a signal for my husband that I was inside the store, still working off my list.

But heaving the thing heavy with a week's food supplies into our pick-up was not what I had meant him to take upon himself.

My dissatisfaction with this solution coincided with another change. Our busses became a lot slimmer back then. Even passengers in wheelchairs didn't find them as roomy anymore. Much less was there space for trolleys like mine. I still used the bus – unless my husband was away jobwise and left me our "wheels" to drive. Yet, I gave up taking my trolley along. I still got picked up by my husband after the weekly groceries. He had to search the aisles for me, now, as the bright blue trolley wasn't parked at the supermarket front desk anymore. I made my environmental statement though. I brought loads of my own cotton bags for shopping. They might not be the latest in fashion statement, but they were sure easier to be loaded inside the truck.

These days, we live near a bus route again, but due to traffic, busses tend to be a bit off-schedule sometimes. Quite a bit. I consider to walk to the stores with my bright-blue trolley again. But our neighborhood boasts no sidewalks – so it's an ordeal, especially in bad weather. I keep thinking of those people who do not even have a chance to ponder when their partner will be able to pick them up or when they may share their wheels. Or of those who are doing groceries on schedule in order to catch the next bus, as they don't have a car. When it's my turn with our wheels, I surely see these people by the roadside with different eyes now.

Citizenship

I was born German, and I am now an American citizen. It sounds easy. And, for me, it probably was in comparison with what other people have to undergo. But it is not as easy as some people think. No, you are not automatically American when you marry an American citizen. It's what quite a few Americans wrongly assume. No, you are not automatically American when you marry a member of the US Forces. In fact, that makes the process even more complex. And, no, it's not easy to have dual citizenship, since mother countries not always pull along with their expats.

What struck me most was the effect emigration has on the people immediately around you before you are about to leave. As much as they try to be happy for you, it is obvious that their pain sometimes outweighs compassion for you who is on tenterhooks about the next step in the process. They don't understand that the waiting might suddenly stop. Friends of mine were shocked when I suddenly received my appointment dates at the US embassy in Frankfurt for the final immigrant visa interview. It was a slap in the face that I didn't make the rounds and visit with everybody before I left my mother country – because there simply wasn't time. It was not that I hadn't told them that this might happen. It was that they didn't want to believe it would.

In fact, during the entire process of hospital checks, paperwork and email exchanges, the personal embassy appointment, the actual arrival at Immigration in SeaTac, and my first paperwork over here, I only ran into the kindest, most helpful American officials. They worked quickly and efficiently. And though it took me almost a year after filing my application for an immigration visa to join my husband, this was faster than the time frame I had been given in the beginning. I was lucky.

It was also clear to me from the start that I wanted to become a US citizen. I knew I'd have to have lived here for a certain period of time to be able to apply for citizenship. And at one point I had to deal with a very discouraging person who told me I'd fail at my first try to become a citizen anyhow. That lady wasn't an immigration officer but a military liaison, by the way, and I might have caught her when she was just headed for her lunch break and her sandwich, which must have been more important than customer service.

For a while I contemplated dual citizenship. But watching German news and following documentaries about dual citizens in Germany failing loyalty to my mother country convinced me that I had to take a stand. I fully appreciate all I have been receiving from this country and the wonderful people who have been crossing my path so far. I wanted to gain the rights and responsibilities of a full citizen here. I am not planning to live in Germany again. My loyalties are here now. I won't forget my roots, but I'm growing new ones here. And they are quite sturdy already.

Filing the paperwork was done quickly. And then I started learning for the immigration interview: history, sociology, politics – 100 questions and answers. And I waited. I'll cut the story short. The authorities were working fast again, and I received my invitation to the pivotal interview in Tukwila quite quickly.

It was a cold December morning in 2017 when I sat in the waiting area of the USCIS building's second floor which seems to be reserved for citizenship procedures. The interview was over in under 30 minutes. My interviewer handed me the paperwork and invitation for the oath ceremony … the same afternoon! It was a rush of emotions I underwent during these last hours before the event, none of them sad. I felt a little dizzy with the speed at which the process was coming to its ending.

And then I was sitting in the auditorium of the USCIS building, along with 68 other people from 41 nations. All kinds of shades and clothing, all kinds of languages. I was sitting between a lady from Poland and a lady from Laos. We stood as we were called up, nation by nation. We spoke the oath, we sang the national anthem, now *our* national anthem, with fervor and tears in our eyes. The grandeur of that moment touched me deeply: To find that 69 people from 41 nations had suddenly become 69 people of one and the same nation … It would never make us a family, it would never weld us as in a melting pot, but it made us a community for that one hour of festive ceremony. What remains are a beautiful certificate – and the memory that immigration is a long, often painful process, but also a rewarding experience. That of finally having come home.

Shoes

Not every woman loves buying shoes. I, for example, am one of those who don't. Though I certainly have enough pairs to complement my diverse styles and color schemes of clothing. What strikes me most these days is how my shoe styles have changed. And how it has been dictated by my lifestyle.

Maybe my dislike for buying shoes leads back to my childhood days. As soon as I entered school, somebody decided I needed special shoes for insoles. My parents, my pediatrician, and some orthopedist, even the shoe sales people seemed to be in cahoots about this. Accordingly, I never ended up with any of the fancy, fun-looking shoes other kids my age used to have, but with shoes that looked awkward and usually came in dreadful colors. As if having to wear specially crafted insoles wasn't insult enough. At one time I howled down an entire shoe department swearing I wouldn't ever wear the shoes my mother had decided I should have. The cartoon book I was given at the cash register didn't sweeten the purchase at all. And, of course, I had to wear the ugly shoes until the next ugly pair was due.

You would think that I was into buying shoes after I had finally outgrown insoles and earned my own money. I wasn't. As I held jobs that required business dress code, I had an abundance of high-heels going with fancy outfits that belied my age. I will never fathom how I walked trade fair floors in stilettos for eight hours at a time, sometimes five days in a row, evening functions not counted in. Somehow my feet seem to have survived this ordeal without growing bunions. Maybe

227

because I started rethinking foot comfort and putting it above shoe looks in my late twenties.

Sneakers though had always been considered a no-go from my childhood on. They were for sports activities only – in my parents' opinion as well as later in mine. And as I was not even trying to pretend to be sporty, I had not a single pair of those in my up-town, upscale shoe cabinet.

Enter: my husband. Place: Washington State.

Have you ever climbed a steep hill in stilettos? Or walked along roads without sidewalks in shoes kind of elegant? Because that was what I brought over here from my mother country, and that is the situation I ran into, often not having a car at my behest. The stilettos were quickly retired, only to be taken out for functions that required evening dress. The other shoes served me well in good weather. But when it rains, roadsides here more often than not get muddy, and puddles quickly grow into lakes. And everybody knows how often it rains in Western Washington.

I finally bought myself some comfortable walking shoes sneaker-style for town walks. Some rustic hiking shoes serve for outings that require firm footing and material resilience, e.g. in the mountains. And my elegant shoes are in use only when I'm able to sit or stand at indoors locations. Lately, my feet seem to have changed shape due to more and more comfortable shoes. I find even one-inch-heel pumps slightly uncomfortable these days, and I keep reducing the number of those. Thrift shops have received most of my European shoes by now.

Still, my shoe rack stays full. I have all kinds of outdoor shoes – for walking, for hiking, for gardening, for boating, for clam digging, for beach walks … Most of them are ugly. All of them are comfortable. And I can't wait for when it will be warm enough again to wear just some fancy flip-flops outside or, when at home, no shoes at all.

Cast-offs

Estate sales are something that I have never been to in my German past. Not that Germany didn't have its number of those – they are usually announced in papers in specific advertising pages. Germany also has thrift shops like Oxfam or Christian organizations' ones. It's just that our family never went to either. We bought new. We saved up to get new. Whereas here in the US, estate sales seem to be a favorite weekend pastime, in Germany it is still associated with poverty. Or being a bit odd. Or ... a collector. At least it was in the circles I used to grow up and live in.

When I came here, I quickly found that getting to estate sales as early as possible was a competitive matter. You see the signs pop up and off you go. Some of those estate sales are professionally organized, others are done by the owners themselves. It keeps astonishing me how many possessions a single household can hold, up to the level of where it makes no sense anymore. I have seen estate sales with three pianos in one room, kitchens with a multitude of rolling pins none of which had intact handles, bedrooms filled with scores of pairs of designer shoes, rusty items in tool sheds that had obviously not been used for ages. I have kept wondering where people stow all these things. And why they keep what they obviously don't use anymore.

I remember that I went over my possessions twice a year way back when and discarded the unusable that hadn't already been disposed to the roadside for the city's biannual bulky waste collection. I discarded clothes that were worn out to clothes containers. I never had more than one rolling pin, one piano, a dozen pair of shoes (which I all wore), and certainly no rusty items. And even now I think I can do without a lot because I simply have no need for it.

Thrift stores are another source of things that one person doesn't want anymore but another might need. Or want. I find so-called antique stores often in a similar department of offers, though there are a few that are really worth looking at for old, beautifully designed furniture or decorative items. A couple of years ago, a friend and I went to a quite fancy antique store in Lakewood in search for a gift for a friend of ours. I saw a couple of gorgeous Japanese ceramic vases that I simply couldn't resist. And that I still have neither room nor purpose for, but they are so beautiful. So, I guess this is how people end up with way more items than a house can theoretically hold.

Sometimes, while wandering around an estate sale, I am more interested in the story the possessions tell about their owners. I spot foreign nationalities, hobbies, tastes, memorabilia of a life that has moved on to somewhere else. I look at the houses and imagine what it must have felt like living in them when there were children's feet pattering up and down the stairs and a dog might have had its bowl somewhere by the backdoor in the kitchen. Estate sales, thrift stores, antique stores are fascinating places to let the mind wander indeed. And I love the thought that things are not just tossed, but that people care about them and buy them for reuse.

I still purge my possessions regularly. Right now, I have an accumulation of bagged vases, seasonal decorations, an unworn sundress (whatever possessed me to buy it?!), and a number of books that I won't reread. They are waiting to be transported to a thrift shop. To imagine that one day anybody would have to handle all the things I use on a daily basis *and* a clutter of items I never even look at … No, I rather take the latter and give them away now. Except the brand-new fondue set that has been sitting unused on a garage shelf - for how many years now? But you never know. I might want to use it yet one day.

Crowned Heads

A few weeks ago, the world was following another British Royal Wedding, and US magazine covers were plastered with the happy young couple. As these pictures slowly fade in our memories, the internet is following suit with images of a brand-new duchess traveling with "the" Queen, and social media are overflowing with people's remarks about her "wild hair" and other comments. Quite a few of them citizens of non-royalist democracies, by the way. So, what is it about the fascination with anybody crowned?

My mother country's aristocracy lost all its entitlements after WW I. There are still a whole lot of people around who have the titles and the property, but nobody talks to them more deferentially than to anybody else. I have sung a solo aria before who would have become Austria's emperor when I was about 16 years old. I had lunch at a private salon with Count Anton-Wolfgang von Faber-Castell at his castle in Stein, Germany. None of them wore insignia at any time. But they had that aristocratic demeanor – and mind me, I don't mean that in a negative way – that would have enabled their heads to bear a crown anytime. Something that made you respect them. Something that made them stand out when they entered a room.

The United States, as we all know, has been a democracy from its very beginning. We call people rather by their given name than by addressing them by their last name and calling them Mister or Miss(is) if we can help it. It's considered more egalitarian. If you want to stand out, do something outstanding. Ah, and here comes the crown!

Well, not everywhere and not at any cost, of course. But when you celebrate a birthday, quite a few people get to wear a paper crown. A famous fast food chain hands out paper crowns to customers celebrating their birthday party at their locations. Western Washington has its daffodil princesses as much as my German county has its wine princesses. High schools have their homecoming queens (and kings), sometimes with an entire court elected by school mates – yes, a crowning ceremony is obligatory. No such thing back in Germany – we have our school speakers and class presidents, the first involved in school policy, the latter being the liaison between a class and their primary teacher. Very democratic, totally without glamor, certainly without any sparkling crowns. And they abdicate with the ending of the senior year – they are simply obsolete after the final exam.

And then, both our democratic nations have their beauty pageants, some for participants who can barely yet toddle, some for young adults, some for seniors. In the end, it is all about receiving a ribbon and wearing a crown, maybe even getting an additional mentioning on your town sign such as "Home of Miss Washington …" followed by the year she received the crown. Ah, to wear that crown … To feel like a princess …

Is that sparkle really all we need to feel special or to dream special? Why do we hanker for stories that involve so much glitter and glamor, even better aristocracy, though we claim we are above and beyond being subjects? Why do we introduce crowns for events into which people are voted or which at best are a birthday?

And then with a jolt we realize that an American citizen has just made our very dream of tinsel and rhinestone crowns her reality. Only that it includes a real crown. Only that she wasn't Cinderella, but already a self-made woman and probably gives up so much personal freedom that nobody seriously would envy her. And let's face it – least of all the weight of a real crown …

Household Items

The other day, I was vacuuming my house and was totally in deep thoughts when, all of a sudden, my vacuum cleaner died on me. The sudden silence woke me out of deep contemplation about a plot twist in my next novel, but I knew immediately what had happened. The plug had fallen out of the plug-in … again. A problem I have come across ever so often meanwhile that dealing with it has become a common measure – bend the contacts either in or out and plug the device in again. In other words, plugs of a lot of US household items don't fit to perfection until you make them that. In Germany, plugged-in means plugged-in – unless you really tug hard and want to run the risk of severing the cable from the plug-head.

Vacuum cleaners – that is another keyword. Back in Germany, I had a nice light-weight drag-behind canister one with big paper bags into which the dust was sucked. Here, in my first years, I carried a really heavy monster – latest model of a well-known brand, mind you – upstairs and downstairs, moving the entire weight of the canister along with my wrist while vacuuming. I simply didn't get the concept. Why would the canister be halfway up the pipe? Why did it take acrobatics-cum-weightlifting to take the appliance apart to either make it reach underneath furniture or to make the canister come apart? What was the advantage of opening and emptying the "anti-allergic" filter and canister over a garbage bin when in a moment I would be covered in the dust I had just vacuumed? Even better, I saw that German friends on Facebook were just proudly announcing they had purchased such a wonder vacuum cleaner. I could only shake the dust out of my hair. After a lengthy search, I found a US-made vacuum cleaner that fit my German standards, by the way. That brand name is the equivalent to a Greek exclamation of joy on finding something. Just saying.

Another fossil is the washing machines that obviously are the most common models, those top loaders with a spindle inside. Don't ask me how many of my family's clothing items have become entangled in the spindle or between the spindle and the bottom and got outright shredded. There must be a secret contract between the producers of such machines and the clothing industry, I'm pretty sure. The only time in Germany I ever ruined clothes was when I accidentally put a red item into a load of white laundry to be boiled. Exactly – the resulting pink was *my* fault. If I wanted to shred something, I'd have had to go to different measures.

And what about all the strangely arranged switches at the back of a stove, so you have to scald your arms while reaching over steaming pots when cooking? Or a hand blender that is falling apart after only five years in all the wrong places, while you're blending, whereas the German thing I used to have was still as good as new after 15 years?

Rant over, because I have a hunch that any American coming over to Germany will have their own little grudges. You will find that in your new German home there are rarely built-in kitchens – yes, you are supposed to design your own. If you are lucky, there's a sink and a stove coming with your rental. Ceiling lights? Those cables in the ceilings are all yours to deal with – or call in an electrician to attach all the lamps you painstakingly bought for your last apartment and that now look lopsided or too long or too short in your new abodes. There are no ACs for hot summers. Forget about washer or dryer coming with your rental – all yours to buy. And telephone and internet services are rarely a pleasure to deal with – not for Germans either, by the way.

Indeed, nothing is ever perfect. Nowhere. All you can do is tell yourself that if everybody else deals with these things, so can you.

I'm still switching on the wrong hobs on my stove top every once in a while, because there is no logic to the array of buttons. Occasionally, I ruin a piece of clothing in the washer – reason enough to get myself or somebody else something pretty and new. I will have to buy a new blender sometime soon and save somebody's job in doing so, I'm sure. But my little vacuum cleaner happily glides behind me everywhere I need it. And, for sure, I have learned to bend plugs.

School Days

What do I remember from my first day of school ever in Germany? A big candy-filled cardboard cone, throngs of people seated in the gym to attend a welcoming program and to listen to the principal, then entering a classroom and being pretty much clueless about anything that was going on. I was able to write my name, count, and read a round, analog (!) clock. That was pretty much it, apart from knowing how to crochet, sew, use scissors, dress and tie my shoes, eat with knife and fork European-style, quote short poems, bicycle, and use public transport. I was six and one of the youngest in my class.

Home was a bit over a mile from school, and after the first few days of being accompanied to school by my mother and picked up later, all on foot, I was left to my own devices. I had a cute umbrella for rainy days, and school was never cancelled when it snowed. It was your own responsibility to be on time -- and you saw to it that you were, for all the classmates screamed, "You're la-ate! You're la-ate!" if you arrived after school had started. There were no school buses. There was public transport, but I rarely received the fare for a ticket. I walked most of my 13 years of school. I think there were a couple of years when I actually used a bike. None of us ever had a car – we were only permitted to drive after age 18 and having passed extensive and expensive driving lessons.

I used to carry satchels. My first one was yellow with a blue dog carrying a flower in its mouth; it had red reflectors for safety. I hated it. My second satchel was brown leather. It looked like … no, let's just say, I hated it even more. I carried loads of books in them to and from school. We had no lockers. We had a place on a shelf in our classroom. One that practically anybody had access to. I rarely put anything in there. We needed to have *all* of our books and study materials at school *and* at home anyhow. Only when I was 15 and came back from my first solitary big trip to the US did I carry a book bag – a beautiful beige canvas one with dark-blue handles embroidered with white whales. It was unique. It stood out like a fashion statement. I loved it.

School started at 7:45 a.m. The first three years we were in school six days a week, after that it was staggered down to finally merely five. Lessons lasted 45 minutes each with a five-minute break afterwards. At 10:10 a.m. we'd have our "big break" – 20 minutes that were used to have a snack. Most kids brought their own from home. Mine always was a sandwich, lovingly wrapped into parchment paper by my mother, and a cut-up apple. Other kids came to school with money and bought baked goods and milk or tea either at the janitor's window or at a table that was set up by a vendor. Lunch was at home. Always. And after homework was done, we were free to roam the neighborhood until dinner or darkness, depending on which was earlier.

Over here, I sometimes wonder where the kids are. Sure, I see them wait for or get off school buses. But I rarely hear or see any outside these times – if I'm not counting toddlers at supermarkets during the day or kids' birthday parties at a venue in a park. I know, of course, that school buses drive everybody collectively to the places they need to be at. So, I don't see anybody of school age walk from A to B. And, of course, I know that kids are staying at school all day more often than not. I admit, it would have driven me crazy as a kid. I remember what torture it was when we were scheduled two afternoons of school per week in third and fourth grade. Later I got over it, but never used to it.

Seeing the school busses and the lines of cars waiting behind, makes me think of how I found it so tough sometimes way back when. The sugar cone on my first day of school lasted only for so long. But ... I'm glad everything was like it was, and I know I wouldn't have envied today's kids their school busses, fancier school fashion, or school lunches. I enjoyed a freedom that children today, in Germany as well as in the US, experience less and less. And if it was only the freedom to pick flowers for my teachers or friends on my way to school or to enjoy running through the neighborhood unsupervised in the afternoons.

Packaging

Sometimes I wonder what it will be like when I'm a couple of decades older, my fingers not as nimble, and my wrists not as strong as now. It usually happens when I'm fighting another packaging of something and I feel that either I am incapable or the package designer totally unempathetic. Also, it is something that hardly ever happened to me back in Germany.

Of course, I had my difficulties opening one or the other German product, too. That occurred e. g. when the rim of a can was higher than my can opener would work; which ended me up with three different can-openers, one of them electric. Or when tiny shards of a bottle neck had worked themselves into the screw top of a bottle, obviously a production or transport accident – I had to use a special jar opener. Once or twice in my almost 42 years over there, I ended up with the lifting ring of a can on my finger instead of with an open lid. But that's pretty much it.

My issues with opening packaging started here almost immediately. Open a big cup of yoghurt – even if you go very carefully and try to detach the aluminum or plastic cover with a slightly circular movement from the rim, you will probably end up with a lid half-ripped and the yogurt from its inner side slapped against your hand. Or tiny mozzarella balls in brine – don't even try to pry the plastic film from the cup. There is simply no other way than to use a knife and cut along the rim. Ruined finger nails ensue when removing the seal on top of a salt box metal dispenser. Ripping lines along zip locks don't rip where they are supposed to be ripping, which either makes you use scissors, after all, or ends you up with a messed-up zip lock. Resealable covers most often don't completely reseal – or they rip in a place that was not even meant to be resealable; I end up piling the contents into household ware. I have fought fights with childproof jars and bottles containing such dangerous stuff as juice or jam – even my jar opener wouldn't work in a couple of cases.

But let's face it – the worst packaging designers seem to have specialized on pharmaceutical products. Apart from having to lean your body weight into the bottle while screwing off its top, by the time you have reached the pills in the bottle, your fingers are stuck in the aperture because you made the mistake of trying to get an entire pound of cotton wool out of the jar. So, you let go of the wad in order to get your fingers out and start the process over again – you need to have pincers to do so. Or these phenomenal packages with tablets in single foil compartments. Either the cardboard-plastic-lining is too thick or I'm too weak – but the tiny cut which you are supposed to "rip open" never works for me. I have to find extra-scissors. Or those ingenious ones where, once you have peeled off the cardboard layer successfully, you find an indomitable layer of foil that prevents you from getting to your medication without a knife. Thick plastic seals around bottle necks with a perforation that doesn't start where you are supposed to rip call for another cutting tool.

I wondering whether these designers ever try their own packaging or whether they don't use the products they design the packaging for. Why make life simple if it can be so much more adventurous, right? Especially when it comes to medication and patients near a heart attack before they reach their pills or drops.

Just the other day, I had to use my teeth to open the packaging of a hiking snack because there was not even the pretense of a ripping line. I didn't really enjoy the taste and feel of plastic in my mouth, not to talk of the thought whose fingers in what condition might have touched the packaging before I did. I'm glad I have healthy teeth and I hope I will still be able to go for long walks even when I have my first tooth replacements or an entire set of dentures. Though I might have to figure a different choice of hiking snacks then. Ones that don't need teeth and nails to be fought open.

Windows

I love cleaning windows. At least I used to back in Germany. Over here – not so much. And that is because window cleaning in the US is so much less gratifying. Not because the windows get less dirty and you wouldn't see the difference. The difference is in the windows themselves.

Germans love their windows open. Even when it's raining or when it's starting to get cold. Maybe that is why you will find tilting windows everywhere. Closed at the bottom, open at the top, they render a room fresh air at all times, usually without any rain getting inside. They also open like doors – mostly to the inside of a room. I do wonder, though, how people clean windows e.g. in the Northern German city of Celle – there the windows of old town houses open to the outside. Which is excellent to obstruct burglars (Clang – take this one into your head, Mister!). But I'd prefer not to hang outside, waist over the sill on a fourth floor, trying to reach the outside pane for cleaning.

Windows over here are certainly less dangerous than those from Celle (unless you count in those cathedral ceilings with floor to ceiling windows or any kind of skylights). For some cases, you simply need professional gear to clean windows thoroughly – but even then, some places escape you. Sliding windows always have parts nobody reaches. Which takes away from my satisfaction. Or you hire a professional window cleaner – but will they take a window apart to reach the places where the frames overlap? I highly doubt it. Also, it's hard to get all the dirt out of the frame. Whenever you move the window over a freshly cleaned place, you can be sure that you reapply dirt from underneath the pane.

Another part of the German window I really miss – window sills. Not just because they are often wide enough to be usable for potted plants (my German kitchen sill used to be an herb garden). They are usually made from sealed marble or granite – which means you can simply wash them down and keep them clean as well.

Is it a wonder Germans love their windows and window sills? I remember some that looked like conservatories. I remember bedding hanging out of windows for airing. Or people spending hours at times hanging out in their windows (windows widely open), making conversation with whoever from the neighborhood passed by. (Here goes the image of the reserved German, right?)

Along with German windows comes a curtain system that I sorely miss. I don't like threading my kitchen curtains over an extendable curtain rod that is weirdly resistant when it comes to putting it back up again. I loved my little wheels that were attached to the curtains even during laundry and that I pushed back into the rails straight under the ceiling. Here, I'm dealing with juggling two and more rods, curtains on, depending on how many layers I prefer at a window. Maybe that is why so many homes here have no curtains at all?

Well, it's time for my fall window cleaning. You want holiday guests to be able to take a look out of the windows, right? I guess I will head out to Lowes and check for more professional window cleaning gear and give it a try. At least, I'm not living on a fourth floor.

Castles

Let's face it: We are all more or less fascinated with castles. In Europe we almost take them for granted. Our ancestors have been exploited during their built. And though the US have managed to break away from aristocracy long before Europeans, there are still quite a few architectural structures that imitate the grandeur of castles, palaces, halls, and aristocratic mansions over here.

One of the most imitated European castles is what so many call Disney castle – probably because "Neuschwanstein" is so hard to pronounce. Actually, it's not. Just try it: Noy-'shvuhn-shtine. There you go! Maybe it's because of its turrets and its (not so unique) location on a rock that people love it so. Also, it looks as if it were from the Middle Ages. It is not. Because, let's face it, most of those medieval structures have been razed by hostile forces in their times. Basically, Neuschwanstein is pretty fake in comparison to other German castles and palaces – and as insignificant. A creation of a 19th century slightly unbalanced Bavarian king with minor historical importance, who used to roam his palaces in solitude.

Other touristy castles are Heidelberg, of course, and Sanssouci in Potsdam. Both played their roles in German history, for sure. And if any of you ever took a cruise on the River Rhine, you will have encountered the numerous castles and ruins on top of the cliffs overlooking the Rhine gorge.

My hometown, Stuttgart, boasts two castles smack-dab in its center. The older one was built in 1292 as a water fortress, and today it is used as the state's museum. And there is a so-called New Castle, built in baroque style, just kitty corner from the old one on the central Schlossplatz (pronounce 'shloss-pluts), i.e. Castle Square. This one is very much in use for official purposes of all kinds, and European royalty sets foot into it quite regularly. As a "normal" citizen you usually get to see only very few rooms of the new castle. Which is why nearby Ludwigsburg Castle gets all the tourism – but we have to be fair: Ludwigsburg's baroque park is as astonishing as its castle's interior. And a further attraction is the fairytale theme park within its boundaries.

Yes, Germany is peppered with the ruins of old fortresses, with old castles, palaces, and mansions. If you'd like to get an impression of what you miss out on while you are still contemplating "Disney Castle" for your next trip, just check out Lakewood author Ed Kane's beautiful book "Roads to Ruins" (www.roadstoruins.com). Maybe you will reconsider your traveling route.

Apropos: Lakewood has its own very beautiful castle, built in Tudor gothic style (though obviously with state-of-the-art sanitary engineering) – Thornewood Castle. It even comes with presidential history. Hollywood used the location for a number of series and movies, amongst them "There Will be Blood" with Daniel Day Lewis. Built as the gift for a bride shortly after 1907, the building and grounds contain ancient elements sold off by British castles and might make you reconsider going to the trouble of traveling to Europe at all, as you can even book a stay there. I have a feeling even the British might be fooled by this fine piece of historical castle architecture.

Whichever – European castles are a bit like our archetypical princess dream, I think. For a moment we step into a world that is unreal. We breathe history. And then we return to enjoy our modern creature comforts.

Acknowledgements

First of all, I'd like to thank Ben Sclair, publisher of "The Suburban Times" in Lakewood, Washington, for giving me the wonderful opportunity of sharing my thoughts on a regular basis in a medium that is much loved by its readership for its reliable publishing and informative contents. More than a few times have I called out for help when I had already submitted an article and found some flaws. Ben always most kindly lent a hand in correcting my mistakes. If you find any in this book, they are all mine.

I'd also like to thank all of those consistent readers and commentators who kept me going and showed me that my idea for this column had hit a nerve. Though "Home from Home" is ending here, I hope to keep Suburban Times readers entertained with further output, currently under the column title "Across the Fence".

And I want to thank my husband, Donald, who, with never-ending patience, kept listening to my ramblings about topical ideas, readers' comments, and circulation for almost two years, read quite a few of my articles, suggested slight changes, and supported me in my writing and publishing in every thinkable way to the point when I disappeared into my writing nook for entire days or almost forgot to make dinner. No writer could fare better.

Made in the USA
Middletown, DE
26 March 2019